ROUTLEDGE LIBRARY EDITIONS:
INTERNATIONAL SECURITY STUDIES

Volume 10

THE INFLUENCE OF BRITISH ARMS

T0382803

THE INFLUENCE OF BRITISH ARMS
An Analysis of British Military Intervention Since 1956

JAMES H. WYLLIE

Routledge
Taylor & Francis Group

LONDON AND NEW YORK

First published in 1984 by George Allen & Unwin (Publishers) Ltd

This edition first published in 2021
by Routledge
2 Park Square, Milton Park, Abingdon, Oxon OX14 4RN

and by Routledge
52 Vanderbilt Avenue, New York, NY 10017

Routledge is an imprint of the Taylor & Francis Group, an informa business

British Library Cataloguing in Publication Data
A catalogue record for this book is available from the British Library

ISBN: 978-0-367-68499-0 (Set)
ISBN: 978-1-00-316169-1 (Set) (ebk)
ISBN: 978-0-367-70157-4 (Volume 10) (hbk)
ISBN: 978-0-367-70159-8 (Volume 10) (pbk)
ISBN: 978-1-00-314483-0 (Volume 10) (ebk)

Publisher's Note
The publisher has gone to great lengths to ensure the quality of this reprint but
points out that some imperfections in the original copies may be apparent.

Disclaimer
The publisher has made every effort to trace copyright holders and would welcome
correspondence from those they have been unable to trace.

The Influence of British Arms
An Analysis of British Military Intervention since 1956

JAMES H. WYLLIE
University of Aberdeen

London
GEORGE ALLEN & UNWIN
Boston   Sydney

George Allen & Unwin (Publishers) Ltd,
40 Museum Street, London WC1A 1LU, UK

George Allen & Unwin (Publishers) Ltd,
Park Lane, Hemel Hempstead, Herts HP2 4TE, UK

Allen & Unwin, Inc.,
9 Winchester Terrace, Winchester, Mass. 01890, USA

George Allen & Unwin Australia Pty Ltd,
8 Napier Street, North Sydney, NSW 2060, Australia

First published in 1984

British Library Cataloguing in Publication Data

Wyllie, James H.
    The influence of British arms.
1. Great Britain—Foreign relations—1945 –
I. Title
327.41   DA45
ISBN 0-04-320161-X

Library of Congress Cataloging in Publication Data

Wyllie, James H.
    The influence of British arms.
Bibliography: p.
Includes index.
1. Great Britain—History, Military—20th century.
2. Great Britain—Foreign relations—1945 – .
3. Great Britain—Military policy. I. Title.
DA69.W95 1984   941.085   83-25830
ISBN 0-04-320161-X

Set in 10 on 11 point Garamond by Red Lion Setters, London WC1
and printed in Great Britain
by Billing and Sons Ltd, London and Worcester

Contents

Contents

List of Abbreviations

ANZUS	Australia, New Zealand and the United States security treaty
BAOR	British Army of the Rhine
BP	British Petroleum
CENTO	Central Treaty Organisation
EEC	European Economic Community
EOKA	National Organisation of Cypriot Fighters
GCC	Gulf Co-operation Council
IISS	International Institute for Strategic Studies
MIRV	Multiple Independently-targeted Re-entry Vehicle
MRV	Multiple Re-entry Vehicle
NATO	North Atlantic Treaty Organisation
OAU	Organisation of African Unity
RAF	Royal Air Force
RDF	Rapid Deployment Force
RM	Royal Marines
RN	Royal Navy
RUSI	Royal United Services Institute for Defence Studies
SACEUR	Supreme Allied Commander Europe
SALT	Strategic Arms Limitation Talks
SAS	Special Air Service
SCUA	Suez Canal Users' Association
SSBN	ballistic-missile submarine, nuclear-powered
TUC	Trades Union Congress
UDI	Unilateral Declaration of Independence
UK	United Kingdom
UN	United Nations
UNFICYP	United Nations force in Cyprus
US	United States
USSR	Union of Soviet Socialist Republics
WP	Warsaw Pact

Preface

The dispatch of military expeditionary forces to faraway, often seemingly exotic places appeals to the atavistic longings of many people and conjures up romantic images. This is especially so if the military instrument is being exercised in support of a cause generally recognised to be worthy, just, or profitable at the time. The use of the military instrument is enhanced if the expeditionary force is successful, or even seen to be successful. But military power is finite, limited, and a complex balance of many forces, and needs to be managed with considerable care. This is so even for the superpowers, and particularly so for democratic medium-rank states in the developed world. Such states are required to husband their expensive military resources carefully, and ought to devote them to only the most worthy objectives.

To many of today's students of international relations, officers in the armed services, public servants, politicians and interested members of the public the international environment may appear fraught with vulnerabilities and dangers to which the military instrument could provide a remedy. The intention of this book is to demonstrate how difficult it has been and how difficult it is for Britain, a medium-rank democratic power, to use the military instrument far from home.

Objectives must be scrutinised and the battlefield carefully selected before recourse to arms is considered as a policy. That was not the case with British policy during the Suez crisis, and 1956 provides an appropriate beginning for this study of British military intervention. Decolonisation was proceeding apace, and conflicts involving young sovereign states were replacing colonial policing as a major role for British military power. In 1956 Britain's international power was found wanting, and the subsequent decade witnessed a painful struggle to carry on as if nothing had happened. Eventually, British security policy was obliged to adapt, but this was a tortuous and painful process. The experience of the use and non-use of the military instrument by Britain in a rapidly growing international system of sovereign states in the years since 1956 must not be overlooked, and should form the basis of any future plans for the projection of British military force into the volatile world outside the relative security of the NATO area. The 1982 Falklands campaign, whilst the most immediate instance of the long-range projection of British military force, constitutes only a part of the experience accumulated since the Suez crisis of 1956.

I would like to acknowledge the encouragement and support of Professor Peter Nailor, Royal Naval College, Greenwich, and Dr Richard Chapman, Reader in Politics, University of Durham, during the writing of this book. My thanks are also due to Mr David Greenwood, Director of the Centre for Defence Studies, University of Aberdeen, and Professor Paul Wilkinson,

Professor of International Relations, University of Aberdeen, for their valuable comments and suggestions regarding the style and substance of this study respectively. I am also grateful to Janice Gordon, Yvonne Rowan-Robinson and Lorna Cardno for the pleasant efficiency with which they typed various drafts. I am, of course, alone responsible for the contents of this book, and for any errors of fact or judgement.

JAMES H. WYLLIE
Aberdeen
January 1983

The Influence of British Arms

Introduction

The Falkland Islands War of 1982 brought the debate over the long-range projection of British military force to the attention of the wider public, but this instance of the use of British military force was not the source of this debate. The source of contemporary interest in long-range military power projection can be traced to the second half of the 1970s, following the shock of the Cuban interventions in Africa, the fall of the Shah of Iran and the Soviet invasion of Afghanistan.

Mounting concern over perceived threats to vital Western markets, trade routes and, not least, sources of raw materials has resulted in a resurrection of interest, in British foreign and defence policy circles, in the projection of British military power beyond the North Atlantic area prescribed by the boundaries of NATO. Continued access to raw materials is of especial concern to the states of West Europe. West Europe is not only vulnerable to a prolonged reduction in the supply of oil but is dependent upon access to a range of other critical strategic minerals such as cobalt, chromium, platinum and manganese. Cobalt has essential aerospace applications, chromium lends firmness and anti-corrosive qualities to stainless steels, platinum is required as a catalyst in the automotive and aerospace industries and manganese is critical as a steel alloy. A considerable portion of these and other vital metals is located in volatile areas of the developing world, and hence consistent Western supplies are vulnerable to disruption and disturbance. For example, most of the non-communist world's output of cobalt comes from Zaire and Zambia and the violent conflict in the Shaba province in 1978 contributed to a quadrupling of the price of Zairean cobalt.

Anxiety in London and in other Western capitals emanates from two major sources. First, it comes from perceptions of Soviet violations of the spirit of détente by building up massive nuclear and conventional military power throughout the 1970s and using that power to underwrite Cuban military adventures in Africa and the expansion of North Vietnam in South-East Asia as well as advancing Moscow's own ambitions in South-West Asia. Secondly, it is generated by internal upheavals in the developing world arising from religious or nationalist feelings, or a mix of both, which are often anti-Western in nature.

British concern and intentions have been articulated.[1] Instruments other than military force, such as development aid and trade policies, have been accorded a role in the pursuit of Western security objectives beyond the North Atlantic. However, despite the outcome of the agonised debates of the 1960s over a role east of Suez, the prospect of the projection of British military power beyond the North Atlantic in the 1980s has not been eschewed:

> The West must make it clear to the Soviet Union and its allies that it is capable of protecting essential interests by military means should the need arise. That task cannot and should not be left to the United States alone.
>
> Against this background, the Government believes that the Services should also be able to operate effectively outside the NATO area, without diminishing our central commitment to the Alliance. British forces will therefore continue to deploy and exercise outside the NATO area from time to time. Moreover, certain improvements in the Services' worldwide capability are being considered.
>
> Such improvements can be achieved at relatively modest cost, yet they give the Services significantly more flexibility to undertake tasks outside the NATO area. What is needed is the ability for all three Services to combine in providing a force of appropriate size and capability as may be necessary.[2]

In the light of such policies it is the purpose of this book to address itself to three major issues and questions. First, it aims to illuminate the political, economic and operational problems associated with military intervention over long distances by a European, democratic, medium-rank state. The Suez crisis illustrated the limits to British political and military power in a most painful manner, and important lessons were learned from the Suez experience – lessons still applicable in the 1980s and 1990s. In the years following Suez Britain exercised its military power far from home on many occasions, and often with considerable success from both the domestic and international perspectives. However, the interventions examined in Chapter 4 were often 'close-run things' and considerable military or political or economic hurdles had to be surmounted.

Secondly, it aims to establish whether Britain, in the final twenty years of the twentieth century, is irrevocably 'out of the business'[3] of military intervention. The Defence Reviews of the second half of the 1960s and the mid-1970s removed many of the essential capabilities required to project major military force outside the NATO area over a prolonged time-scale but, as the Falklands War graphically illustrated, a tradition, a propensity and in many cases an expertise – military and bureaucratic – remains within the British defence establishment if a regular military role beyond the North Atlantic had to be revived.

Thirdly, it aims to suggest that, although West European medium-rank powers – perhaps in collaboration, and strictly following the ground-rules established by Britain since 1956 – could intervene militarily beyond the North Atlantic in a limited fashion, there are other more cost-effective and politically acceptable and manageable ways by which West European powers could make political and military contributions to international security commensurate with their economic power and status.

These issues and questions are primarily of interest not because of the threat to residual West European colonial responsibilities posed by irredentist Third World powers equipped with some modern weaponry, but because of the apparently increasing vulnerability of pro-Western states to internal, and externally inspired and supported, insurrection, turmoil and on occasions near-anarchy. The events in the Shaba province of Zaire in 1977 and 1978 stand as an illustration of the utility of the long-range projection of limited and moderate military force by West European states at the invitation, and in support, of the legitimate government.[4] Not only is Shaba province the source of supply for most of West Europe's cobalt and much of its uranium, but, of great import to democratic Western states, the lives of many West European citizens were at risk. As the Iranian Revolution demonstrated, it is far from inconceivable that threats of a similar or greater nature could recur not only in Africa but in the Middle East as the rule rather than the exception, rooted in the social, political, economic and religious growing pains of rapid modernisation. It could be argued that the mere presence of a West European military capability to come to the aid of modernising states, if invited, could have a stabilising effect. Furthermore, it could also be argued that some counter is required to Soviet and Cuban adventurism in areas peripheral to West Europe (even more so to the Soviet Union) but none the less of strategic significance. This is especially so as the United States temporary post-Vietnam reluctance to fulfil an international policing role appears to have been cast off. In search of Alliance support Washington has argued, with some justification, that as, for example, Middle Eastern oil is more important to the economy of West Europe than to the economy of the United States, the West European states ought to bear more of the 'stability-inducing' burden. In 1981 Secretary of State Alexander Haig reflected this view in an interview with *Der Stern*:

> During my entire period in Europe, I spoke about the dangers of Third World developments, not just to the United States but to the NATO Alliance as a whole; and I also repeatedly made the point that whether or not NATO was concerned about Third World developments, it was going to be affected by them in any event.
>
> I have always felt that our ability and will to deal with intervention in the Third World, outside the formal NATO framework, was in fact the work of the Alliance, because it contributed to the security of all the member governments of the Alliance.
>
> In many respects Third World developments today are of even more crucial strategic importance to European members of the Alliance than they are to the United States. I would particularly be concerned about energy, but it also includes other increasingly important and increasingly scarce raw materials as well.[5]

How best can Britain, and its West European partners, respond to such a call, and what guidance is provided by the British experience of military interventions since 1956?

Notes: Introduction

1 See *Defence in the 1980s. Statement on the Defence Estimates 1980, Volume I*, Cmnd 7826–1 (London: HMSO, 1980), Ch. 4; *Statement on Defence Estimates 1981, Volume I*, Cmnd 8212–1 (London: HMSO, 1981), Ch. 1, p. 5, para. 11; and *The United Kingdom Defence Programme: The Way Forward*, Cmnd 8288 (London: HMSO, 1981), p. 11, para. 32.
2 *Defence in the 1980s*, op. cit., paras 408–10.
3 Pierre Lellouche and Dominique Moisi, 'French policy in Africa: a lonely battle against destabilisation', *International Security*, vol. 3, no. 4 (1979), p. 131, fn. 71.
4 See Peter Mangold, 'Shaba I and Shaba II', *Survival*, vol. XXI, no. 3 (1979), pp. 107–15.
5 'Interview: Secretary of State Haig in *Der Stern*', *United States International Communication Agency* (London, 21 August 1981).

1 The Military Instrument, Britain and Intervention

Before pursuing answers to the questions posed in the Introduction it is essential to establish the following premises:

(1) That, in the contemporary world, despite the advent of nuclear weapons, the exercise of military power and force continues to be accepted as a meaningful, worthwhile component and in certain circumstances an extension of diplomacy. The acceptability of military force as a diplomatic instrument by Western liberal democratic states, and especially West European medium-rank powers, is of particular interest. If West European states have abandoned the military option, leaving the exercise of such options to the superpowers (or one superpower), or to less developed, non-democratic states, waging local conflicts, then this examination of the British experience is pointless.

(2) That Britain in the period under study is a medium-rank power in the European context, and hence a proper subject of study.

(3) That as the intervention option outside the NATO area is the focus of this study, the British experience can be accurately defined as intervention. Intervention is a term much abused by the international media, so much so as to render the concept nearly meaningless. A popular view of intervention has arisen which more or less equates it with any degree of involvement in, or comment upon, another state's affairs, ranging from the provision of economic aid to the pronouncements of American presidents on human rights in the Soviet Union. In this study a more rigorous and precise definition of intervention will be adopted, and applied to the British experience.

The Military Instrument as a Diplomatic Option

The term 'power', and its components such as economic power and military power, are used on a daily basis by statesmen, journalists, academics and other commentators on the political scene, domestic and international. One can adopt a 'rule of thumb' approach to power, apparently rational, by arguing that State A has capabilities X, Y and Z, which State B does not possess in such abundance; that these attributes are recognised as important elements of power, for instance, a large modern army or a sophisticated industrial base; so consequently State A is more powerful than State B. In many cases such rough assessments and general definitions of power are adequate but, in contemporary history, there are notable instances of misconceived conceptualisations of what constitutes power, and mistaken assessments of power: for instance, British action during the Suez crisis of 1956 and United States involvement in Vietnam. Power is essentially a descriptive term and ought to be used to describe a specific relationship rather than as a general all-embracing term:

> Power is really a relationship. By this is meant that we cannot know whether a nation was powerful until we can relate its actions to the ends which it sought, to its resources and capacity, to the existence of opposition and the perceptions of the policy maker. Modest aims may be framed by those responsible for political decisions, and achieved, while those more ambitious may only achieve a proportion of their objectives. Both cases involve the exercise of political judgement based upon an awareness of the international context and national resources, together with some idea of what is considered desirable. But only when such ends are clearly stated and achieved (or not) can any evaluation of power have any meaning.[1]

Nevertheless, perceptions of power, including military power, whether meaningful or not – perceptions which are often based upon a crude 'awareness of the international context and national resources' – have been a major factor in the judgements and decisions of innumerable statesmen for centuries. If power can be defined as the capability of a state to make its will felt in the decision-making process of another state then, 'a state may be said to have power in the international system when another state recognises that it cannot be ignored when issues have to be determined'.[2] This power reflects, among other things, the capability to use force. It can be argued that military force is the checklist of military capabilities and its implementation signifies the breakdown of military power. In many cases, when one can assume rational decision-making, the use of military force illustrates a form of psychological weakness in that a state cannot achieve its objectives through the threat of force but only through its implementation, that is, the target state was not convinced of the superior power of its adversary.[3] One could apply this rule to Britain's relations with Indonesia during the 'Confrontation' years of 1963–6. British military power was such that Indonesia could not be deterred from its actions against Malaysia, to which Britain had given public defence assurances, with subsequent resort to the use of British arms. It is important to note that the difference between the use of force and the use of violence is the higher degree of legitimacy of the former. One can draw a distinction by arguing that violence is carried out by non-governmental agencies, for instance, terrorist groups, not acting on behalf of the state as instruments of state policy. This assumes, of course, a *de jure* government, and in some cases this may be a highly emotive, contentious matter.

It is generally acknowledged that, with the development of the nation-state in the nineteenth century, a state's armed forces perform other, often vital functions in addition to the exercise of military power in pursuit of foreign policy objectives. The development of military power may be the result of a plethora of interrelated interests:

> governments may value military forces for the purpose of internal control and security rather than international deployment. The maintenance of military forces may be to the advantage of particular career and business interests, or lend support to national economic prosperity and growth. In a good many countries the armed services are often called upon to perform such non military tasks as harvesting crops and fighting floods and forest fires. The armed services may be cherished as a repository of past military glory, regarded as a symbol of national unity, and appreciated as part of the system of education and social integration and mobilisation.[4]

However, normally, in Western democratic societies and also in the less democratic states in the international system, military power fulfils, primarily, an external function unless there is severe civil disruption. The main reason why states have found themselves unable to dispense with military power is because the international system is essentially anarchic. Security is the central problem of international politics and the primary objective of each state in its external relations is the preservation of itself as a state and the pursuit of interests which contribute towards that objective. Ultimately, each state is responsible for its own security and, as history testifies, military force is frequently the final arbiter of relations between competing states. Most statesmen, no matter how well intentioned, are aware of the amoral nature of the international system. As an illustration of this hard fact of international life, Michael Howard identifies Attlee, Cripps, Wilmot and Noel-Baker as men who had little sympathy with the politics of power and who spoke publicly against it in the 1930s, but who in the 1950s saw it as essential to protect democratic values: 'This realisation of the impotence of ethical principle to operate unaided in a world of power does much to explain the speed with which the world rearmed after 1950.'[5] The search for security and the ability of states to control their immediate environment, or even an environment geographically far removed, are the most decisive influences on foreign and defence policy-making. The attention and resources that even traditional, or legally based, neutral states devote to their armed forces and defences emphasise the following statement:

> Any sovereign state – that is, any community which wishes to maintain a capacity for independent political action – may have to use or indicate its capacity and readiness to use force – functional and purposeful violence – to protect itself against coercion by other states. Given the state system, peace is possible only when there is freedom from all fear of coercion; and

in the absence of any supranational authority enforcing a universal rule of law, such freedom from fear still depends at least partly on independent or collective military capability.[6]

Alliance is one way of reducing the burden of military power, or compensating for a lack of military power, and is particularly popular with Western governments which have large electorates demanding more resources for social welfare. But to be attractive as an alliance partner and to maintain an influential voice within the alliance there must be some meaningful contribution of military power. It is often claimed that Britain's influential voice in the councils of NATO is a function not merely of history but, more important, of large British forces on the Continent and, as some sectors of British political life would argue, the British Polaris force.

By the late 1960s and early 1970s, very much as a result of the United States experience in Vietnam and the apparent superpower nuclear deadlock, military power and the use of force, excepting the nuclear deterrent role, was seen to be increasingly redundant by many people in the Western industrialised democracies. The deterrent function of many modern weapons systems in addition to the general feeling that the use of violence, albeit by the state, was an immoral and perhaps illegitimate way to achieve foreign policy objectives contributed to this trend. The failure of the United States and British governments to attract the required numbers of personnel to all-volunteer forces when there was relatively full employment in their domestic economies, and the clear unfashionability of aspects of society associated with the military in countries such as Japan, West Germany and the Netherlands, bear witness to this trend. With rising living standards and the low profile of any external threat, issues of domestic politics such as social welfare and the distribution of wealth assumed an unmistakable priority in the affairs of the democratic Western states, particularly in West Europe. In the early 1970s Stanley Hoffmann described Western democratic societies' view of the exercise of military force thus: 'They are societies in which citizens want what Constant described as 'le repos et l'aisance' instead of glory, what de Tocqueville called higher status and standard of living instead of turmoil.'[7] In the years since the painful experience of early postwar decolonisation there has been a marked reluctance on the part of many Western powers, particularly West European medium-rank powers, to use military force as an instrument of foreign policy. This stems, in all probability, from the experiences of two world wars and the often bloody process of postwar decolonisation, a recognition of the uncontrollable nature of military conflict once in motion, the vast expense of war-making and the realisation that trade and investment are the route to success (the bulk of international trade being between developed countries anyway) rather than military conquest. By the early 1970s many Western countries, in contrast to the 1950s and 1960s, refused to accept that any conflict in faraway parts of the international system was a threat to their vital interests:

the system's tolerance for conflict was higher than had been thought, and the danger of nuclear war more remote. As societies began to understand that their interests and values were not in fact at stake in every distant contingency they became increasingly relaxed – if not agnostic – about the preservation of peace throughout the system.[8]

Hoffmann writes of the consumerist-, internationalist- and welfare-oriented nature of modern liberal democracies – all anti-militaristic movements – but he warns of the potentiality of modern industrial states to make ideal garrison states, for which there is ample evidence in the two world wars of this century.

However, questions of security, defence and military power have tended to be debated among an informed elite. Only with the immediate prospect of casualties and large public expenditure do such matters become the province of public debate and then, as the United States experience in South-East Asia illustrated, it is exceptionally difficult to educate a democracy to accept limited war: 'War in a democracy required demonification of the enemy, and demonification is quite incompatible with limits.'[9] It is difficult to persuade public opinion that limited objectives are worth limited casualties, particularly if the conflict continues for more than a few weeks; for instance, the public mood in Britain over the Falklands conflict stands in sharp contrast to public indifference and some widespread hostility to the British army's presence in Northern Ireland. In the early 1970s the prevalent feeling was that, except as a deterrent, military power as an instrument of foreign policy had lost much of its usefulness. The contemporary configuration of international relations was such that the use of military force to achieve foreign policy objectives was no longer a viable option.[10] Indeed, in the extra-European world, military power was fulfilling a more purposeful role within states rather than between states.

Nevertheless, 'power' remains in common usage among international statesmen, advisers and bureaucrats as a crude measure of a state's potential influence and authority *vis-à-vis* other states. The concept of military power suffers from the same intellectual objections as power but in the world of real, practical politics the concept retains a healthy high profile. The influence of perceptions of military power is probably more important in the twentieth century than ever before and this state of affairs looks likely to continue into the twenty-first century.

The power which states exercise in international affairs is compounded of many attributes, economic, diplomatic, cultural, and ideological as well as military. But military power, the capacity to use violence for the protection, enforcement or extension of authority, remains an instrument with which no state has yet found it possible completely to dispense.[11]

Writing in 1975, John Vincent uses the examples of the Turkish-Greek conflict, the Israeli-Arab conflict, the wars in South-East Asia and also the British experience in Northern Ireland to argue that

> The idea that both the utility and legitimacy of force have declined is a Western one which has small correspondence with experience outside the West, and has, furthermore, to be severely qualified in order accurately to render Western experience.[12]

Although one can draw a hazy distinction between the concepts of power and influence, the distinction is not at all clear and, as a consequence, power is often equated with influence over the actions of others – the relational concept.[13] But, although military power does not always equal political influence – the more a state spends on arms does not mean a proportional increase in influence – it would be foolish to deny that there is a relationship of sorts. States often increase armaments and accept vast politico-military diminishing returns for every extra tank or missile produced or purchased in order to increase political influence, no matter how amorphous. The political influence argument was used by the Conservative administration of 1959–64 as the main plank in the platform supporting the retention of a British nuclear deterrent. Similar arguments were used by the Labour government in its attempts to maintain British forces in bases east of Suez prior to sterling's devaluation in 1968.

That decision-makers in target states are aware of the increase of the components of military power on the other side of the border, or on the surrounding oceans, is illustrated by many examples throughout history, not least the contemporary history of West Europe since 1945. The glowering presence of the Red Army and Warsaw Pact forces has influenced the foreign policies and often the domestic politics of nearly all West European states, though not always in the preferred direction. The continuing build-up of Warsaw Pact forces throughout the 1970s together with periodic doubts about the United States commitment to Europe, particularly in terms of expensive conventional forces, has, despite détente, raised fears of 'Finlandisation' in the minds of many West Europeans.

Nuclear weapons, at the superpower level, are no exception to this crude relationship. Superpower nuclear relations and political attitudes to nuclear weapons best illustrate the relationship between military power and political influence. The Soviet Union, in a successful attempt to achieve superpower equivalence with the United States through the medium of military power, has severely strained its economy, and now faces a host of socio-economic problems caused, to a considerable extent, by its extravagant defence expenditure.[14] Nevertheless, in the eyes of most states the Soviet Union is a superpower to whose opinions great importance must be attached and, often, deference given. The illustration of superpower status, as perceived by the Soviet hierarchy and numerous observers, was the agreement by the United States to conduct bilateral negotiations with the Soviet Union over matters of national security, that is, SALT. In the world of international affairs perceptions of power and influence wielded by others as well as themselves, drawn by statesmen often with little technico-military expertise, are frequently based on impressions, and large nuclear arsenals are very impressive.

However, in the contemporary world the exercise of power in a military dimension is by no means limited to the projection of power via the passive exploitation of nuclear stockpiles. The number and frequency of military conflicts around the world illustrate that military force is still utilised, in many forms, as an extension of diplomacy:

> Military force can sometimes be used to achieve an objective forcibly, without persuasion or intimidation; usually, though – throughout history but particularly now – military potential is used to influence other countries, their government or their peoples, by the harm it could do to them. It may be used skilfully or clumsily, and it can be used for evil or in self-protection, even in the pursuit of peace; but used as bargaining power it is part of diplomacy – the uglier, more negative, less civilised part of diplomacy – nevertheless diplomacy.[15]

In the context of conventional armaments, recent Soviet incursions into Africa, for instance, in Angola and Ethiopia, albeit by proxy with 20,000 and 17,000 Soviet-supplied Cuban troops respectively, and the occupation of Afghanistan, illustrate the continuing utility of military force.[16] It has been estimated that on every single day of the thirty-two years between 1945 and 1977, 11·5 wars (armed conflict) were in progress and that the total duration of the wars fought since 1945 (up to 1977) adds up to more than 369 years. The most common conflict is the internal anti-regime war, with foreign participation.[17] Soviet success in Africa and South-West Asia and the inability of the West to respond appear to vindicate a warning made by Laurence Martin in 1973:

> if views of both acceptability and utility were changing in an asymmetrical way among the nations of the world . . . a sense of unacceptability sufficiently high to encourage an attitude of appeasement in one power would increase the utility of force for another.[18]

However, the actual use of military force since 1945 has on the whole, apart from traditional colonial policing, been limited to either the superpowers or Third World powers. In the Third World the frequency of intrastate conflicts exceeds interstate conflict to a considerable extent,[19] owing to the instability of the governments of some of the recently founded states and the doubtful legitimacy of the incumbent government in the eyes of some sections of the population. Violence in the Third World is not subject to the same restraints traditionally associated with Western society. Often the principal issue in Third World struggles is not the guaranteeing of the state's security but the making of a nation. Nevertheless, these intra-state conflicts often have international implications, for instance, the Nigerian Civil War caused conflict within the OAU, political argument within Britain, friction between France and Britain and provided an opportunity for Soviet involvement in West African affairs.

Following the short hiatus of the early post-Vietnam years, there appears to be a resurgence in the acceptability of the use of military power in some sectors of West European public opinion. It could be that, at last, feelings of 'imperial guilt' are subsiding or that the post-1973 economic recession, the behaviour of some Third World states (politically as well as economically) and the perceived reawakening of Soviet 'imperial' ambitions have 'toughened up' Western electorates; for instance, support for the Belgian-French intervention with United States logistic support in Kolwezi, Zaire, in May 1978. This action was remarkably successful and, particularly in the case of France, raised the prestige of the government both nationally and internationally.[20] Throughout the West press reaction was on the whole favourable and in France public opinion supported the intervention.[21]

Since Kolwezi, France has been strengthening the parachute and marine forces which form the core of its intervention capabilities. In a television interview in June 1979 President Giscard d'Estaing stated that 'should they be faced with a situation affecting their very life, industrial Western countries might be forced to have reactions proportionate to this change'.[22]

The fact that the United States, to which West Europe usually looks for a lead, created a special task force to respond to crises in vital areas of the Third World before the impetus provided to the Rapid Deployment Force concept by the Soviet invasion of Afghanistan is indicative of the change of mood in some quarters:

The armed forces are a popular cause again in America: defence spending is up: and the defence secretary can even talk about a 'unilateral force' – may it please be given a decent name? – without fear of being ridden out of town on a rail.

The causes of this turn-around are not hard to find. The passing of time since the Vietnam War ended, and the boat people's evidence of what a Communist Indochina is like, have begun to change the conventional wisdom about that unsuccessful but dishonourable American intervention. More important, American opinion has been shaken by the growing evidence that a dozen years of Soviet rearmament have given Russia not only nuclear equality with America (or more than equality) but also the ability to organise vigorous non-nuclear military action in far-flung corners of the world. Add the Cuban expeditionary force in Africa, and a packet of East German advisers, and the case for a western counter-intervention force – contemporary equivalent of the 'fleet in being' – is evident. France has one, and is strengthening it; America needs one too.[23]

In addition, the continual pressure emanating from NATO on the need to counter Soviet adventurism which threatens Western lifelines keeps the question of the exercise of military power to the fore in the minds of the foreign policy public in West Europe.

In recent years instruments of foreign policy for democratic countries such as West Germany, the Netherlands, Italy, Japan, Canada, Australia and New Zealand (except for the incursion into Vietnam in the company of a superpower) can be seen to be preponderantly non-military. In addition to the reasons given above, this could be explained in part by the availability to Western societies of many non-military means of pressure such as economic pressure, extensive propaganda capabilities, arms sales, suspension of diplomatic relations and withdrawal from international organisations. Such non-military means of pursuing foreign policy objectives, to which developed Western states traditionally have greater access than the Soviet bloc states and the less-developed countries, lower the value of military power.

Indeed, the developing power of the commodity states following the October War of 1973 and the increasingly diverse sources of military and economic aid have somewhat reduced the effectiveness of the traditional non-military instruments of foreign policy upon which medium-rank powers have relied for many years. It is against this international backdrop, together with an upsurge of Soviet expansionism in the Third World, that the exercise of the military instrument in foreign policy has come back into vogue in the West.

Britain as a Military Power

In 1945 Britain was generally recognised and accepted as a world power. Military power was not excluded from these calculations. In 1948, three years after the cessation of hostilities with the Axis powers, Britain had 940,000 men under arms,[24] a defence budget of £692·6 million[25] and military bases and commitments strung across the globe. Today, more than thirty years later, Britain is recognised as a European medium-rank power. Within official circles in Britain this fact of international life was not acknowledged until 1969 when the Duncan Report announced that Britain was now 'a major power of the second order'.[26] One can identify a real transformation taking place a few years before the Duncan Report, in the years 1956–63: the failure at Suez, the inability to procure domestically a credible nuclear weapons delivery system, wholesale decolonisation and the swift about-turn towards Europe in an attempt to gain economic security and salvage an international role, albeit initially unsuccessfully, all signalled a real decline in Britain's influence and status in the international system.

In the military sphere, Britain disposed of relatively more firepower in 1982 than at any time since the Second World War though it had only 343,000 men and women under arms, 62 major combat surface vessels, and about 700 combat aircraft.[27] But Britain is no longer in the same military league as the United States and the Soviet Union. The United States has over 2 million men under arms, and the Soviet Union has over 3·5 million men (excluding 500,000 internal security, railroad and construction troops). The United States has 201 major combat surface vessels and the Soviet Union has 294 combat surface vessels. The United States has about 5,000 combat aircraft, the Soviet Union has well over 5,000.[28] Britain does possess nuclear weapons but, in total terms, British nuclear firepower is minute compared with that of the two superpowers.

A rough comparison of defence budgets (NATO definition) reveals Britain's military peer group. The United States defence budget in 1981−2 was $171 billion; Britain's defence budget was $28·66 billion; France's defence budget was $26 billion; the Federal Republic of Germany's defence budget was $25 billion; the Netherlands, with a quarter of Britain's population, had a 1981−2 defence budget of $4·93 billion; Denmark, with one-tenth of Britain's population, had a defence budget of $1·52 billion.[29] Such figures illustrate that, in the context of the developed world, Britain is a medium-rank European military power.

Though highly trained and armed with sophisticated weapons, British conventional forces are operationally 'Eurocentric'. Following the decision to withdraw from mainland bases east of Suez, considerable significance was attached to Britain's special contribution to the defence of the flanks of NATO.[30] However, within five years the role of British military power in, and contribution to, this defence role, particularly on the southern flank, was being seriously questioned. The lengthy review of British defence policy undertaken by the Labour government which entered office in 1974 resulted in a concentration of British military power in 'the areas where Britain can best contribute'.[31] The Central Region of NATO, the eastern Atlantic and Channel areas, the security of the United Kingdom and its immediate approaches and the British contributions to the NATO nuclear deterrent were to be the foci of attention for British defence planners. The 1974 White Paper announced the reduction of specialist reinforcement forces for the flanks of NATO.[32] These decisions weakened reinforcement capabilities available for defence of the northern flank while the decision to withdraw from Malta by 1979, reduce forces in Cyprus and discontinue the allocation of maritime forces to NATO in the Mediterranean meant the virtual abandonment of a southern flank role for British forces. By the 1980s, in geo-military terms, Britain was not simply a European military power, but a military power with a predominantly central, continental perspective.

At first sight the Polaris nuclear submarine force, and any chosen successor system, would appear to elevate Britain above most of its European contemporaries excluding France, but in today's climate of world opinion can one ever imagine the threat of the deterrent being credible outside the European context? It is highly unlikely that the United States or Britain's EEC and NATO European partners would tolerate the use of Britain's nuclear weapons in the unilateral pursuit of foreign policy objectives. It should be noted that the Polaris force was of little utility in deterring the Argentinian invasion of the Falkland Islands in 1982; neither did it contribute to the expulsion of the invaders from the islands. As it is, geography and the present level of British strategic nuclear weapons technology restrict the operational scope considerably. Owing to the densely populated nature of the British Isles, the proximity of large industrial and military complexes to large British cities and the fact that the accuracy of the MRVed (but unMIRVed) British Polaris warheads is limited, Britain cannot contemplate a strategic nuclear graduated deterrence scenario. Acting independently, Britain can only follow some kind of counter-city strategy and this appears worthwhile only if national survival is at stake. In such a context and against the backdrop of ever-developing superpower weapons technology, the diplomatic significance of the British possession of strategic nuclear weapons, as distinct from battlefield tactical nuclear weapons, is open to question.

In the essential economic and technological components which, *inter alia*, contribute to an assessment of power in general and military power in particular, imprecise though such an assessment may be, Britain's position as a medium-rank power appears to be confirmed. Table 1.1 gives some comparative GDP figures.[33]

Table 1.1 *Comparative GDP Figures, 1980*

	GDP 1980 ($US)
West Germany	792
France	632
Japan	976 (GNP)
Netherlands	154
Britain	485

This relative decline of Britain's military power is not a phenomenon of the 1970s but has been following a steady and decisive course since the early postwar years when the economic and psychological exhaustion caused by being an unconquered belligerent for all six years of the Second World War prevented Britain from exploiting all the economic and political opportunities presented in the years of reconstruction; see Table 1.2.[34]

As suggested above, a mere tabulation of wide-ranging capabilities is a

Table 1.2 *World Economic Balance (GNP in $US billion)*

Year	USA	Japan	West Germany	France	UK	USSR
1952	350	16	32	29	44	113
1960	511	39	71	60	72	201
1966	748	102	123	108	107	288
1972	1,152	317	229	224	128	439

crude method of assessing power. There are important, intangible elements which contribute towards, or indeed subtract from, a state's power. One of the most important of these intangible elements is the will to exercise influence in the international system. In the early years of the twentieth century the United States, which on any crude economic, naval, technological and demographic reckoning ought to have been considered one of the great powers, was not included in the same league as Britain, France and Germany. The United States lacked the will. The same could be said, perhaps, of Japan in the contemporary world. However, in the years since 1945 it is beyond doubt that Britain has possessed the will to exercise influence in the international system, but increasingly and severely lacked the capabilities.

Britain: a Case Study of Military Intervention

The exercise of military power, particularly in the affairs of other sovereign states, is popularly recognised to be the near-prerogative of the superpowers or their proxies, or of developing countries engaged in local conflicts of limited interest to the developed world. Invasions for the purposes of conquest and annexation have become a rare spectacle in the years since 1945. The exercise of military power, in a direct manner, has manifested itself predominantly in terms of military intervention. United States military involvement in South-East Asia in the 1960s and early 1970s, the use of Soviet military power in disciplining its 'independent' East European satellites and invading Afghanistan, the use of military force by the Indian government in support of East Pakistan (Bangladesh) nationalists against the West Pakistan authorities and the Tanzanian military intervention in Uganda in 1979 are frequently quoted examples of military interventions and have contributed to the images many people hold of what sort of country intervenes with military power, and in what circumstances.

There are three main contributing factors which help to explain the plethora of interventions over the past three decades:

(i) the proliferation of new nation-states, most of which were not considered capable of maintaining their own independence,
(ii) the existence of a sharp ideological cleavage between the two superpowers which precipitated attempts to gain support from the new states, and,
(iii) the production of nuclear weapons which eliminated the possibility of war between the two major actors and encouraged them to employ subversive tactics and, often, proxy forces on battlefields far from home territory.[35]

The above factors help to explain the involvement and high profile of the United States in many of the postwar military interventions. Through action and rhetoric the United States gained the image of being the world's police-man. In 1962 John F. Kennedy stated that 'for the next ten or twenty years the burden will be placed completely on our country for the preservation of freedom'.[36] His successor, Lyndon Johnson, declared at a Lincoln Day dinner in 1965, 'History and our own achievements have thrust upon us the principal responsibility for the protection of freedom on earth'.[37] The Demo-cratic administrations of the United States in the 1960s were inclined to see military intervention by United States marines throughout a disturbed and ideologically confused Third World as a kind of twentieth-century 'Manifest Destiny' for which the United States had been specially prepared and for which it was specially equipped.

In the years since 1956, and in a deliberately much less publicised man-ner, Britain has been involved in a number of military interventions. This is surprising and worthy of note when one bears in mind the traumas suffered because of the ill-advised use of military force during the Suez crisis. It is also worthy of note because British action was one of the major exceptions to the rule that democratic medium-rank powers avoid the use of military force in relations with other states. The other major and continuing exception to this rule has been France:

> Africa is a continent from where traditionally, a certain number of our resources as well as a certain number of raw materials come, and with which we have very close links, and Africa, even if remote for many Frenchmen, is the continent neighbouring ours. So that a change in the political situation in Africa, a general situation of insecurity, subversion in Africa, would have consequences for France and Europe.[38]

French military intervention has occurred only in Africa in francophone states, usually former colonies, with which France has maintained excep-tionally close cultural, economic and formal defence relations.[39] Neverthe-less, the French experience does make a major contribution to the West European pool of knowledge concerning the projection of military power overseas.

British interventions are mainly explained by the first contributing factor mentioned above. Many of the interventions were not the result of state versus state, but the result of internal struggles for power and influence within, or the inherent instability of, new nation-states. It would be mistaken to argue that no British politicians had a vision of an international peace-keeping role for Britain. Some did, from both main political parties, but their ideas were rarely as grandiose as those of the Kennedy and Johnson adminis-trations. Moreover, as the 1960s passed it soon became obvious that Britain could no longer afford to go it alone in such ventures. The United States gained an unpopular image from its high profile interventionary role. Despite 1956, when the United States contributed to international opinion condemn-ing the Anglo-French intervention at Suez, Britain did not gain an unpopular image outside the non-communist world from its intervention activities – an illustration of the dynamics of international politics!

This being the case, is it correct to describe British actions as intervention? Would terms such as military assistance or military aid not be more apt rather than classifying British actions in the same category as those of the United States? To settle this question the concept of intervention needs to be examined closely and related to the instances when British military force was used outside British sovereign territory in the years since 1956.

The term intervention can be used to describe numerous activities in the international system, often with very little in common. As part of political rhetoric and propaganda, intervention is often used to describe one state's interest in or relations with other states. Under such a loose blanket term, Marshall Aid could have been called intervention, Chinese railways and agricultural projects in various African states could be called intervention, United States pronouncements on human rights in the Soviet Union can be, and often are, labelled as intervention. As James Rosenau has stated: 'Ambiguous and contradictory formulations characterise the voluminous moral, legal and strategic writings on the subject, and as a result, intervention has come to be treated as synonymous with influence.'[40]

A definition of intervention is important but difficult. As Rosenau has noted, precise definition has become confused through usage of the term. Intervention tends to be used as an operational concept by diplomats and strategists who are seeking a convenient descriptive term while political scientists seek to use it as an analytical tool. Rosenau argues that the commonsense usage of the term is too wide and 'allows for any action towards another nation to be regarded as intervention'.[41] As K. J. Holsti comments: 'If we classify as intervention all actions that may have some impact immediately or in the long run on another state's internal politics, then today virtually all forms of persuasion and diplomatic-economic-military programs would qualify.'[42] From this perspective intervention no longer constitutes a special event in international relations but could be used to describe any conventional transaction between governments. Obviously this is inadequate as, for example, the infiltration of guerrillas from one state into another and the acceptance of foreign aid are very different sorts of relationship. In an attempt to give some meaning to the term, Rosenau proposes a more precise definition:

> Stated briefly, all kinds of observers from a wide variety of perspectives seem inclined to describe the behaviour of one international actor towards another as interventionary whenever the form of behaviour constitutes a sharp break with then existing forms and whenever it is directed at changing or preserving the structure of political authority in the target society.[43]

Rosenau warns that not all sharp breaks should be regarded as interventionary. The authority-oriented nature of the action is important – to be defined as 'interventionary' the goal of the action should be essentially political. The sudden decision by one state to pursue an aggressive commercial programme to capture a substantial part of the market in another state should not be treated as an example of intervention.[44] British behaviour towards a number of states in the period under consideration conforms to Rosenau's two prime characteristics of intervention. To these two characteristics Holsti would add a third: 'Most, but not all, of the unconventional actions are taken without the consent of the legitimate (e.g. commonly recognised) government.'[45] Since 1956, Britain does not conform to Holsti's perception of the third characteristic that identifies most interventions. But the escape clause – 'Most, but not all' – allows British actions to come under the umbrella of Holsti's additional, third characteristic as well as Rosenau's two authority-oriented, essentially political characteristics. One should note that since 1956 British governments have gone to great lengths to establish the consent of the legitimate, host government in any interventionary situation.

Intervention in the affairs of other states can take many forms. Military intervention is one of the higher profile forms of intervention and can express itself in different ways:

> Intervention is a type of activity, and there are also types of intervention. Military intervention might be one such type, taking place when troops are despatched to keep order or to support a revolution in a foreign state, or when military aid is given to a government whose internal position is insecure or which is in conflict with a neighbouring state. It has also been argued that the very presence or display of armed force, such as the location of the American Sixth Fleet in the Mediterranean Sea, has an effect on the politics of the littoral states tantamount to intervention in their affairs.[46]

Military intervention can be used to maintain or rectify the balance of power, and may assume defensive or offensive forms.[47] Defensive intervention aims at the preservation of a particular regime or system. Examples of defensive intervention include Soviet intervention in Hungary in 1956 to protect the Kadar regime and United States intervention in Lebanon in 1958 in support of the Shamoun administration. Since 1956 British military intervention has only been defensive, for instance, in support of King Hussein's government in Jordan in 1958 and in support of the Emir Abdullah of Kuwait in 1961.

To warrant the descriptive term intervention the temporary nature of the action is important. The longer military forces remain, the less unconventional the behaviour becomes, for instance, as with Soviet forces in Czechoslovakia since 1968. A status of occupation, conquest, or perhaps alliance is then perceived to exist. 'Intervention is a temporary and finite phenomena',[48] and must be seen in the first place to break conventional forms of behaviour and then to facilitate a return to the ante-intervention situation.

Since 1956 the British government of the day has gone to great pains to ensure the temporary nature of its military action.

Matters of the legitimacy and the moral nature of their actions have been of the utmost concern to British governments when contemplating military intervention in the years since Suez. Such concerns do not invalidate the use of the term intervention but in practice restrict military interventions to a particular type, that is, defensive, and to specific situations, that is, when actions are legitimised by treaty and/or requested by the legitimate government. Furthermore, concern over the moral nature of their actions has led British governments, whenever possible, to establish a firm basis of opinion and bipartisan political support in favour of British military action. Where this has been lacking, governments have been reluctant to use military intervention as a way of achieving foreign policy objectives, for instance, over the Rhodesian rebellion in 1965.

These issues of legitimacy and morality are important, especially in a democratic state, but they are often confused. Morgenthau adopts a *realpolitik* perspective which rejects the idea that intervention should be based on moral criteria as, in the final analysis, principles are abstract and often nebulous. He argues that intervention should be related to a state's direct interests and nothing else. If intervention is in the state's direct interests then, *ipso facto*, the action is legitimate.[49]

However, assuming that a state has a unanimous perception of its self-interest, the issue of legitimacy often concerns more than one state's perception of self-interest. In these days of instant communication international public opinion is important and can often influence domestic public opinion. The highest profile and most voluble indicator of international public opinion is the United Nations General Assembly. United Nations approval and a favourable world opinion are viewed by many as a legitimising force.

Even in totalitarian societies the issue of legitimacy, for both domestic and international public consumption, is of supreme importance, for instance, the attempt to legitimise the military intervention in Czechoslovakia in August 1968 by the announcement of the Brezhnev Doctrine and the concept of a Socialist Commonwealth. Joseph Frankel argues that intervention has come to be deemed permissible as long as vague legal forms are followed – the intervening state was invited by the government in power or by a 'liberation' movement.[50] British actions have conformed to Frankel's first precondition. Writing in 1973 Frankel identified the new Third World states as supporting the latter precondition as a legitimising force, and ascribes this to the 'national self-determination' principle prevalent among Third World nationalist groups. However, as these nationalist groups have become established in power and the often unnatural frontiers of former colonies have gained some historical continuity, particularly in Africa, this view may have changed completely. The OAU adopts a very hostile stance towards external intervention in the affairs of African states other than those with a ruling class of European stock.

From the above analysis of what constitutes intervention in general and military intervention in particular and from the discussion of instances of British military intervention since 1956 which will follow in subsequent chapters, it can be seen that it is correct to define these instances of the exercise of British military force as military intervention. British military intervention abides by Rosenau's two characteristics and is not invalidated by Holsti's additional third characteristic. The legitimacy and defensive nature of British action do not preclude use of the descriptive term intervention. British military intervention was of a temporary nature and forces were usually withdrawn very quickly.

Since 1956 Britain has intervened with military force in the affairs of many states – usually former colonial territories or states with which Britain had an imperial relationship. If these countries had still been colonies the use of the term intervention would be incorrect. The description 'colonial policing' would be apt and this is totally different from intervention.

Britain did not wish to become involved in foreign entanglements but, despite Suez, it felt obliged to become involved – a function of its perceived world role, residual imperial responsibility and, often, treaty obligations. Nevertheless, military force was always employed reluctantly with the express and explicit desire to return to non-military means of implementing policy as soon as possible. Mention of Britain and military intervention together lead most people to think of the Suez crisis of 1956 – a classic case of intervention: hostile, aimed at changing the policy of the target government (or perhaps changing the government itself), of questionable legitimacy in the eyes of much of domestic and international public opinion and with strong suggestions of duplicity on the part of the political leadership. However, the many instances of British military intervention since Suez do not correspond with this classic, aggressive and unsuccessful model; yet these actions were still well within the parameters of what most commentators would describe as military intervention. Indeed, there is no other term which describes adequately British action in, for example, Kuwait in 1961, Cyprus in 1963 and East Africa in 1964. Ironically, the Suez crisis, which was seen by many as an illustration of the decline of British power, led on the whole to a more carefully considered and successful use of British military force (though this in itself can be viewed as a decline in military power) outside continental Europe and outside British sovereign territory.

Notes: Chapter 1

1 Charles Reynolds, *Theory and Explanation in International Politics* (London: Martin Robertson, 1975), p. 84.
2 F. S. Northedge, 'The resort to arms', in F. S. Northedge (ed.), *The Use of Force in International Relations* (London: Faber, 1974), p. 101.
3 See Philip Reynolds, *An Introduction to International Relations* (London: Longman, 1975), p. 116.

4 Klaus Knorr, *On the Uses of Military Power in the Nuclear Age* (Princeton, NJ: Princeton University Press, 1966), p. 7.

5 Michael Howard, 'Ethics and power in international policy', *International Affairs*, vol. 53, no. 3 (1977), p. 369.

6 Michael Howard, 'The relevance of traditional strategy', *Foreign Affairs*, vol. 51, no. 2 (1973), p. 253.

7 Stanley Hoffmann, 'The acceptability of military force', in *Force in Modern Societies: Its Place in International Politics*, Adelphi Paper No. 102 (London: IISS, 1973), p. 3.

8 David C. Gompert, 'Constraints of military power: lessons of the past decade', in *The Diffusion of Power*, Adelphi Paper No. 133 (London: IISS, 1977), p. 4.

9 Hoffmann, op. cit., p. 6.

10 For example, see Adrian Guelke, 'Force, intervention and internal conflict', in Northedge (ed.), op. cit., p. 101.

11 Michael Howard, 'Military power and international order', *International Affairs*, vol. 40, no. 3 (1964), p. 405.

12 R. J. Vincent, *Military Power and Political Influence: The Soviet Union and Western Europe*, Adelphi Paper No. 119 (London: IISS, 1975), p. 4.

13 See Joseph Frankel, *International Politics, Conflict and Harmony* (Harmondsworth: Penguin, 1973), pp. 118–19.

14 For an interesting and succinct analysis of this paradox of Soviet politics, see Robin Edmonds, *Soviet Foreign Policy 1962–1973, The Paradox of Super Power* (London: Oxford University Press, 1977).

15 Thomas C. Schelling, *Arms and Influence* (New Haven, Conn., and London: Yale University Press, 1973), p. vi.

16 See *Strategic Survey 1978* (London: IISS, 1979), pp. 12–17.

17 See Istvan Kende, 'Wars of ten years (1967–1976)', *Journal of Peace Research*, vol. XV, no. 2 (1978), p. 228. See also Istvan Kende, 'Twenty five years of local wars', *Journal of Peace Research*, vol. 8, no. 1 (1971), pp. 5–22. It should be noted that wars are defined very broadly.

18 Laurence Martin, 'The utility of military force', in *Force in Modern Societies: Its Place in International Politics*, Adelphi Paper No. 102 (London: IISS, 1973), p. 14.

19 In the decade up to 1966 there were over '149 serious internal insurgencies' in the Third World. This figure was quoted by Robert McNamara during an address to the American Society of Newspaper Editors, Montreal, Canada, 8 May 1966, quoted in Richard J. Barnet, *Intervention and Revolution* (London: Paladin, 1972), p. 16.

20 See Pierre Lellouche and Dominique Moisi, 'French policy in Africa: a lonely battle against destabilisation', *International Security*, vol. 3, no. 4 (1979), p.123.

21 ibid., footnotes 41 (Press reaction) and 39 (public opinion).

22 'New French force for trouble spots', *Guardian*, 27 June 1979.

23 See 'The gleam in Brown's eye', *The Economist*, 30 June 1979, p. 14.

24 *Statement Relating to Defence 1948*, Cmnd 7327 (London: HMSO, 1948), p. 3, para. 10.

25 ibid., p. 4, para. 20.

26 *Report of the Review Committee on Overseas Representation 1968–1969*, Cmnd 4107 (London: HMSO, 1969), p. 22.

27 *The Military Balance 1981–1982* (London: IISS, 1982).

28 ibid.

29 ibid.

30 For example, see General Sir Walter Walker, 'The challenge in the north', *NATO's Fifteen Nations*, vol. 16, no. 2 (1971), pp. 44–50.

31 *Statement of Defence Estimates 1975*, Cmnd 5976 (London: HMSO, 1975), ch. 1, p. 9, para. 25.

32 See ibid., pp. 10–13, paras 26–9. See also Lawrence Freedman, 'Britain's contribution to NATO', *International Affairs*, vol. 54, no. 1 (1978), pp. 30–47.

33 *The Military Balance 1981–1982*, op. cit.

34 *The Military Balance 1973–1974* (London: IISS, 1973), p. 79.

35 Richard Little, *Intervention. External Involvement in Civil Wars* (London: Martin Robertson, 1975), p. 7.
36 Statement of John F. Kennedy, 28 August 1962, reported in the *New York Times*, 29 August 1962, quoted in Richard J. Barnet, op. cit., pp. 24–5.
37 Address of Lyndon Johnson, 12 February 1965, reported in the *New York Times*, 13 February 1965, quoted in Richard Barnet, ibid., p. 24.
38 News conference by Giscard d'Estaing, reported in the *Observer*, 17 April 1977, and quoted in Peter Mangold, 'Shaba I and Shaba II', *Survival*, May/June 1979, p. 110.
39 See Lellouche and Moisi, op. cit.; Mangold, op. cit.; and James O. Goldsborough, 'Paris dateline: Africa's policeman', *Foreign Policy*, no. 33 (Winter 1978/9), pp. 174–90.
40 James N. Rosenau, 'The concept of intervention', *Journal of International Affairs*, vol. XVII, no. 2 (1968), p. 166.
41 ibid.
42 K. J. Holsti, *International Politics, A Framework for Analysis* (London: Prentice-Hall, 1974), p. 278.
43 Rosenau, op. cit., p. 167.
44 See ibid., p. 169. For a list of the advantages gained by using the two prime characteristics of intervention as a basis for operationalising the concept, see pp. 169–70.
45 Holsti, op. cit., p. 279.
46 R. J. Vincent, *Nonintervention and International Order* (Princeton, NJ: Princeton University Press, 1974), p. 9.
47 See Charles O. Lerche, Jr, and Abdul A. Said, *Concepts of International Politics* (Englewood Cliffs, NJ: Prentice-Hall, 1970), pp. 116–17.
48 Rosenau, op. cit., p. 167.
49 See H. J. Morgenthau, 'To intervene or not to intervene', *Foreign Affairs*, vol. 45, no. 3 (1967), pp. 425–36.
50 See Frankel, op. cit., pp. 158–9.

2 Suez 1956: How and When Not to Intervene

History does not repeat itself, but it has much to teach us, especially about what not to do.[1]

In 1956, for reasons of high diplomacy and grand strategy, control over the Suez Canal and the security of the short route to India were perceived to be as vital a national interest as in Britain's imperial heyday. From the late nineteenth century, and through two world wars, Britain waged lengthy and costly campaigns to secure Egypt and the Suez Canal. Even by the 1950s, and in a world much changed from the days of Kitchener's campaign in the Sudan, British governments perceived partial ownership of the canal and freedom of navigation through the canal as a vital national interest, irrespective of the independence of both Egypt and India. In 1956 many British colonies still existed beyond the Suez Canal, and economic and strategic interests appeared to demand a British presence east of Port Said: 'Britain in 1956 still ran half Africa. The word "Empire" was hardly yet anachronistic'.[2]

In addition to the more traditional British national interests in the Middle East three other factors came into play in the postwar years. First, the economies and the military machines of the West, including the United States, were becoming increasingly dependent upon Middle East oil. Secondly, there was widespread fear and apprehension of communist subversion and influence in this vulnerable and volatile part of the developing world. Thirdly, since 1948 the new state of Israel, in a situation of perpetual hostility with its Arab neighbours, was a constant source of potential instability and regional conflict.

These three factors accounted for the interest of Britain's major ally, the United States, in the region. Anti-imperialist, with a strong sector of public support for Israel, yet attempting to implement a policy of containment in the Middle East by way of a strong alliance of Arab states together with former West European colonial powers, the United States found itself pursuing a very complex and delicate foreign policy in the Middle East in the 1950s. By 1956 the United States was deeply involved in a region outside its traditional geographical area of interest.

A major effort by Paris, London and Washington to enhance stability in the region was through arms control. The Tripartite Declaration in 1950[3] pledged France, Britain and the United States to defend whichever side became the victim of aggression from the other in the Arab-Israeli dispute, and in an attempt to manage the hostility all three powers provided military aid to the Arab states and Israel, but only sufficient to maintain a military balance.[4] In 1954, following Britain's decision (encouraged by the United States) to withdraw from the Canal Zone, the United States offered aid to Nasser to facilitate the Egyptian purchase of American military equipment but, in pursuit of non-aligned status, Nasser declined. Later in 1955, following an upsurge in Egyptian-Israeli hostility, Nasser requested United States military aid but, in the absence of adequate funds, the Egyptian request was not successful. Cairo's threat to look to the communist world for military aid was not taken seriously but in September 1955 the announcement of a Cairo–Prague arms deal surprised the West. The by-passing of the Tripartite powers meant not only the failure of the West's security policy via arms control for that part of the Middle East, but a strengthening of the fears concerning communist influence in that region prevalent in Western capitals.

Containment of the perceived communist threat underlay United States support of and British involvement in the Baghdad Pact of 1955. However, the history of Anglo-French colonialism created suspicions among the Arab states over Western motives in encouraging the alliance. The Baghdad Pact may have served a containment function *vis-à-vis* Moscow but it exacerbated the West's poor relations with Egypt and encouraged radical Arab nationalism rather than subduing it.

Following the hostile response to the Baghdad Pact and the opening up of an Egyptian-Soviet bloc arms trade, the Western powers decided to attempt to counter communist influence through the offer of economic aid specifically for the development of the Aswan High Dam. In late 1955 the United States quietly offered to join Britain and the World Bank in financing the dam – a project of great political significance to Nasser.

It was hoped that the prospect of Aswan Dam finance could be used as an instrument to tempt Nasser away from his developing relations with the Soviet bloc. Britain was always doubtful over the economic value of the project but concurred with the United States in the wish to keep Moscow out of Egyptian and Middle Eastern affairs as much as possible. Nasser, however, was most reluctant to accept the terms of the Western loan as it would have resulted in the direction of the Egyptian economy by the World Bank. With no sign of Nasser reducing his contacts with Moscow, with negotiations over the terms of the loan becoming increasingly difficult and with London expressing reservations about the whole project, Dulles, on 19 July 1956, met Nasser's envoy and informed him of the withdrawal of United States support. *Inter alia*, Egyptian relations with the Soviet Union were a major reason for the withdrawal of United States support,[5] as was revealed in a letter from Dulles to Eisenhower in September 1956: 'of course Egypt, in its flirtations with the Soviet Union, had itself consciously jeopardised our sharing in this project, and they had tried to bluff us by pretending to [accept] Soviet "offers" '.[6]

Whatever the reasons for the United States withdrawal, it provided the pretext on 26 July for Nasser to announce the nationalisation of the Suez Canal in an effort to raise the funds for the Aswan Dam project. The British government held 44 per cent of the shares in the Suez Canal Company and in 1955 28.3 per cent of all the tonnage passing through the canal had been British.[7] The canal yielded over £30 million a year in profits. Nationalisation raised all sorts of legal issues regarding the 1888 Convention and the 1954 Suez Base Treaty while there were grave doubts over Cairo's ability to pay compensation, but rational considerations were far outweighed in London by sheer emotional outrage:

> The British were seized by a spasm of anger, none more than the Prime Minister. For them as for all Western Europe, the canal was an essential artery of trade. Among other things, a great part of their oil imports came through it. To many sober citizens – Cabinet Ministers, men in the street, leader writers of the London 'Times' – 'Egyptian' spelt 'incompetent': ships would run aground, the banks would cave, the bottom would silt up. For Englishmen, moreover, and especially for Tories, the Canal had connotations apart from commerce. It was visibly symbolic: Empire, Disraeli. Nasser, furthermore, was violating treaties in the manner of the dictators twenty years before. The parallel seemed striking: every Minister had memories; none more so than Stanley Baldwin's Foreign Secretary, now Prime Minister.[8]

Paris was equally enraged by the Egyptian nationalisation of the canal, not only as France had a large stake in the Canal Company but also because Nasser was thought to be actively engaged in supporting the Algerian rebels in their bloody campaign against the French army and colonists.

As history has recorded, just over three months after the nationalisation of the canal, following much public international diplomacy and domestic debate, British and French armies in apparent collusion with Israel contrived to intervene in the Arab-Israeli War of 1956 under the pretext of protecting an international waterway – the Suez Canal. Politically the action was a disaster, while militarily it can only be claimed to have been a partial success. Anglo-American relations were severely strained, though quickly repaired; Franco-American relations were strained even further and perhaps have never completely recovered; British credibility as a beneficent decolonising world power was greatly diminished; British influence in the Middle East declined; Soviet influence, supported by Moscow's truculence towards London and Paris during the intervention, albeit declaratory, was strengthened; and the Suez intervention detracted from the propaganda opportunity offered to the West by the other, simultaneous, international crisis – the bloody suppression by the Soviet Union of the uprising in Hungary.

The Suez intervention demonstrated not only the limitation of British forces but also intellectual confusion over their use. After Suez, in a world where Britain was not the military power it had imagined itself to be a short time before and in an expanding system of independent developing states, some of the intellectual fog was lifting. The direction of British defence policy was not changing (unlike the French) – Britain still had global responsibilities and commitments and wished to continue a global role – but the Suez fiasco served to caution British governments over the difficulties of future independent, classical military interventions, particularly if the support or approval of Britain's major ally is absent.

The effects of the Suez crisis on British morale were surprisingly temporary and the British government recovered quickly despite (or because of) the loss of a prime minister. Changes took place in the British force structure, as illustrated by the Sandys White Paper of 1957,[9] but commitments remained. Indeed, as Empire changed into Commonwealth, defence agreements with former colonies usually closely followed independence and, irrespective of legal obligations, British governments invariably experienced feelings of residual imperial responsibility. In the decade following Suez British forces found themselves intervening, with considerable political and military success though not without risk, east of Suez. However, in these instances British forces were not operating in the intellectual fog of 1956. Suez illustrated when not to intervene and certain ground-rules for successful intervention, particularly by Western, democratic, medium-rank powers, arise from the British experience in the Suez crisis of 1956. Five identifiable interrelated guidelines for successful intervention emerge from the Suez experience:

(1) There should be a strong domestic and international moral base for the action.
(2) The intervening state should have its action legitimised by invitation from the sovereign power or by international legal obligation.
(3) If intervention is undertaken then military capabilities must be adequate and used as quickly as possible.
(4) The approval and co-operation, or at least absence of opposition, of the United States is essential.
(5) A clear realistic and realisable political objective – the fundamental maxim of the use of force – is essential, and once it has been achieved military forces should be withdrawn quickly.

An examination of the Suez experience in the light of these 'rules' of intervention illustrates the interventionary lessons to be learned from that fateful operation.

Moral Basis

British support, albeit of a limited nature, for Jewish immigration into Palestine and the final abandonment of the United Nations mandate in 1948 perpetuated the distrust of British motives in the Middle East prevalent among the Arab nations since the early post-First World War imperial days. The attempt to control security and maintain the fragile and, in Arab eyes, unfair status quo by Britain, France and the United States through the Tripartite Declaration, which 'laid down the principle that applications for arms should be considered only "in the light of legitimate self-defence and . . . defence of the area as a whole" '[10] increased antagonism towards the West which was perceived as pro-Israeli and unlikely to come to the aid of the Arab states should Israel undertake aggression.

British support for the Baghdad Pact of 1955 heightened Arab suspicions. Turkey and Greece had joined NATO in 1951 and in an effort to extend and spread containment the Arab League was urged by Washington and London to join an Anglo-American Middle East defence pact. Nasser was against this suggestion as he saw his freedom in foreign policy being curtailed and Egypt becoming a possible target for Soviet subversion, while Nuri of Iraq, in competition with Nasser for leadership of the Arab world, supported the plan. In 1955 Iraq formed a defence pact with Turkey, supported by Britain which still had airfields in Iraq. France and the United States, however, having established the level of Arab hostility, were unwilling to support the Baghdad Pact publicly for fear of antagonising Arab opinion further. The result of the pact was in fact an upsurge in Egyptian hostility, the Egyptians claiming that the pact was another illustration of British intrigue. Furthermore, the pact was seen as a divisive factor in Arab unity against Israel:

> before the pact was signed Nasser seemed genuinely poised in indecision on the issue of commitment to the West . . . the pact, by once more kindling suspicion of British intrigue, precipitated him into the neutralism into which he was being induced at the Bandeong conference of African and Asian states at the very time when Britain adhered to the pact.[11]

By 1956 there was precious little Arab sympathy upon which Britain could draw in the Middle East. Meanwhile Egypt had discovered a source of arms in the Soviet bloc.

In addition to there being little sympathy for Britain in the Middle East, internationally there was little support for British outrage over the nationalisation of the canal or for subsequent British actions. Anti-colonialism is one of the few Third World unifying factors and British actions during the crisis certainly appeared 'imperialistic'. Military intervention was greeted with almost unanimous disapproval by the Third World, while all of the Commonwealth except Australia and New Zealand opposed the use of military force. As Hugh Thomas comments, midway through the crisis, in August, most of international opinion aligned with Dulles's idea for an international board to administer the canal. Most of the international community had come to perceive the crisis as 'fundamentally a business dispute over the control of an international public utility in a monopolistic position'.[12] The elevation of this 'business dispute' into an international military crisis did not persuade the international community to support the British view. Needless to say Moscow was critical of Britain's stance from the beginning of the crisis, and 'rocket-rattling' by Bulganin during the intervention, when Moscow threatened to attack London and Paris if there was not a military withdrawal, though improbable, did harden opinion against Britain, especially in the extra-European world where the Soviet Union gained considerable prestige. Ironically, Britain more than France was the butt of international opinion. Apparently much better behaviour was expected of Britain.

International opinion was further aggravated by the perceptions of Anglo-French-Israeli collusion over the attack on Egypt. Arab, particularly Egyptian, hostility towards the state of Israel and constant border skirmishing meant that the possibility of war between Egypt and Israel was ever-present. The hostility of Nasser, the infusion of Soviet bloc arms and the border battles – despite some notable Israeli successes which in turn upset the Arab states even more – worried the Israeli government of Ben Gurion and a preventive war appeared attractive, especially if French, and perhaps British, support was forthcoming. At this time the French government of Guy Mollet saw the existence of the Fourth Republic as dependent upon the success of French arms against the rebels in Algeria. As Nasser was believed to be supporting the rebels with military aid, Suez provided an ideal opportunity to remove his presence from the Algerian problem.

Circumstantial evidence and memoirs and analyses published since 1956 strongly support the accusations of Anglo-French-Israeli collusion.[13] On 3 October Eden gained Cabinet approval to use British military force in a peace-keeping capacity if Israel attacked Egypt but he already knew that French-Israeli talks had been taking place and plans had been drawn up for action contingent upon British support. It appears that from the middle of October secret Anglo-French-Israeli discussions were taking place culminating in a high-level meeting at Sèvres, a Paris suburb, which included Selwyn Lloyd, Ben Gurion, Dayan and Peres. On 23 October the likelihood of war between Israel and an Arab coalition was heightened by the formation of the Arab United Command. The secret cover story prepared between Britain, France and Israel was that Israel would attack Egypt in the Sinai Peninsula and Britain and France would intervene to protect the canal.

Whatever the historical debate, and most professional historians come down on the side of collusion,[14] the events of the time as they happened conveyed a firm impression to the world at large of disreputable collusion and put Britain in an impossible moral position, especially at the United Nations where Britain used its veto in the Security Council for the first time.

On 29 October Israel attacked Egypt but some British vessels had put to sea on the 28th, ostensibly for exercises, while intelligence reports had been used as the excuse for putting some forces on alert. On the 30th Britain and France issued ultimatums to both Egyptian and Israeli forces to withdraw ten miles east and west respectively, threatening intervention unless a twelve-hour deadline was observed. Israel could comply and still leave forces one hundred miles inside Egyptian territory. Egypt, of course, refused to withdraw. The United States was surprised, as it expected joint action with the British and French as agreed by the Tripartite Declaration, but this was not to be. On 31 October Britain and France blocked a Security Council resolution calling for an Israeli withdrawal and on that same day bombardment of Egyptian airfields by the RAF began, and continued for five days. On 2 November the United Nations General Assembly adopted a United States resolution against force by sixty-five to five (only New Zealand and Australia joined Britain, France and Israel), while there were six abstentions, including Canada. On 3 November Egypt announced acceptance of the UN demand for a ceasefire and the following day Israel indicated a willingness to do likewise. Israel had achieved all its objectives but the Anglo-French invasion force had not yet arrived. To continue the pretext for the invasion, France put pressure on Israel to impose conditions on any ceasefire acceptance. On 5 November Anglo-French paratroopers dropped on Egypt and on 6 November the invasion finally began.

Such a contrived set of circumstances produced deepseated and reasonable suspicions of Anglo-French-Israeli collusion. Britain's credibility in the international community sank to an all-time low, and the moral base for British action was generally perceived to be non-existent.

Even more debilitating for a state engaged in hostilities and with international opinion running strongly against it was the state of public opinion at home. British public and official opinion was divided. Initially there was great outrage but as time passed opposition to the use of force arose. The Labour Party quickly came to see the United Nations as the proper instrument with which to manage the crisis[15] and the TUC was similarly against the use of force. Splits appeared in the ranks of the Conservative Party which *inter alia* may explain Eden's support for a negotiated settlement in the early days of the crisis and for the idea of the Suez Canal Users' Association later, though he never rejected the use of force as an instrument. On 27 July, the day following the nationalisation of the canal, the Chiefs of Staff were instructed to prepare a military plan. From the beginning the Chiefs of Staff, including the First Sea Lord, Earl Mountbatten,[16] were most unenthusiastic, as was Monckton, the Minister of Defence. The reservations were political as well as military. The Foreign Office, although Kirkpatrick (the Permanent Under Secretary) supported Eden, expressed great concern over the effects of the use of force on the Anglo-American relationship and British influence in the Arab world. Eden, however, appeared convinced that Britain should use force unilaterally if necessary and if all other instruments failed. Nasser's action reminded not only Eden but many in the British foreign policy establishment and the public at large of the actions of Hitler and Mussolini in the 1930s.[17] For many who ought to have known better, Egypt was cast in the same mould as Nazi Germany and Fascist Italy or perhaps, as F. S. Northedge suggests, the violent reaction to the canal nationalisation emerged from an unconscious residue of resentment against the decline of British power, the dissolution of Empire and the transfer of the leadership of the Western world to the United States.[18]

In foreign affairs Eden was predominant in Cabinet, Selwyn Lloyd being a very inexperienced foreign secretary in sharp contrast to Eden's record and prestige in the field of foreign policy. Furthermore, there was domestic pressure on Eden to prove himself a tough prime minister. A section of the Conservative Party felt he had 'lost' Egypt in 1954 while the government's inability to resolve the Cyprus troubles did not reflect well on the Eden administration. Over the Suez crisis figures such as Macmillan and Salisbury pushed for strong action and supported Eden's interpretation, while moderates such as Butler and Monckton found they could not influence the Prime Minister. Indeed, by 18 October Monckton resigned as Minister of Defence, ostensibly on grounds of poor health.

When Israel attacked Egypt and the Tripartite Declaration was not implemented and the British veto was used at the United Nations, a deep division of opinion in the country revealed itself. Gaitskell and the Labour Party were indignant over lack of consultation on such an important national matter. The separation of combatants pretext was seen as a charade.

The middle classes of both major political persuasions were, on the whole, critical. The *Guardian* had opposed the government's line from the beginning while, once military force was used, there was 'hostility from nearly all the Press, including the *Telegraph* and the *Daily Mail*; the *Express* and the *Sketch* were Eden's only real newspaper friends. *The Times* had crossed over.'[19]

Favourable public opinion, international and domestic, is a very important instrument in the armoury of every state, particularly a democratic state, contemplating the large-scale employment of military force to achieve a foreign policy objective. Nevertheless, this is not to say that inadequate public support was the only reason for the failure of the Suez intervention. Public opinion regarding the morality and the appropriateness of the British actions was one factor among others – 'to insist that the failure of Suez must be found in the power of world public opinion is to push a door that is already open'[20] – but, beyond doubt, it was a very important and major determinant of events, not least because as the opposition of public opinion to Eden's policy came to be appreciated the resolve of the Egyptian government strengthened.

Legitimacy

A factor of great importance, and one which vitally affects public opinion, is that of the legitimacy of an intervention. If there is a sound basis in international law for the intervention or the intervention is clearly the result of an invitation by the sovereign government then the opinions of interested governments and publics are much less likely to run against the policy of the interventionary power.

Was the nationalisation of the canal illegal? Was there any legitimacy in the demands for international control of the canal? The British legal position was uncertain and this factor, as well as the fact that legal action is a lengthy process, appear to have been the basis of Britain's reluctance to go immediately to the United Nations or the International Court.[21] In strictly legal terms Nasser had nationalised the Suez Canal Company, not the canal. The company, though its headquarters were in Paris and its shareholders were mostly British or French with only five Egyptian directors, was actually an Egyptian company. The company's rights in Egypt were legally decided by a series of 'concessions' reaffirmed by Nasser not long before nationalisation but the Egyptian government, as a sovereign state, could abrogate them. The canal was guaranteed as an international waterway by the Treaty of Constantinople in 1888. If Egypt had proved itself incapable of running it then it would have been in breach of that treaty. However, Egypt ran the canal quite well despite British expectations to the contrary.

Legality was on Britain's side on one issue. Egypt was in breach of the Treaty of Constantinople by not allowing Israeli ships passage but this had been the case since 1951, and no firm action had been taken. Anyway, the intervention appeared somewhat pointless as the Canal Company's concession ran out in 1968, twelve years later, when ownership of all facilities would pass to Egypt. The refusal of the British government to put Nasser's nationalisation of the canal to the legal test severely weakened its claim that Nasser's action was contrary to international law. The Suez Canal Base Treaty of 1954 hardly legitimised British intervention. Under the treaty Britain agreed to withdraw forces from the canal base within twenty months but installations were to be maintained by British and Egyptian civilians and the base could be reactivated in the event of an armed attack on Egypt or any other member of the Arab League or Turkey. However, although Israel's attack against Egypt on 29 October would have legitimised any British request to reactivate the canal base it certainly did not legitimise any British military attack against the sovereign state of Egypt or British demands that Egypt withdraw ten miles from the canal. There was no invitation to intervene and there was no treaty which legitimised intervention. The British intervention against Egypt in 1956 was clearly illegal and none of the requirements described above was present, unless one insists that the nationalisation of an Egyptian company by the Egyptian government was an act of aggression:

> the justifiability of . . . intervention is properly an international question to be decided by international procedures according to international law. As treaties now generally prohibit forceful intervention except for defence against armed attack, there is a presumption against the legitimacy of such action unless expressly permitted by a protectorate, mandate, or trusteeship,

or other treaty relations with the state in whose territory the action is taken or unless that state has been found guilty of aggression which withdraws it from the benefits of antiwar treaties and permits military sanctions against it.[22]

The Charter of the United Nations clearly condemns the threat or use of force in international relations with the sole exception of self-defence against armed attack. In the mid-1950s many people still had great faith in the United Nations and the fact that Britain's action was contrary to the Charter detracted even further from the legitimacy of the intervention. There were those who argued from the heart that Suez was a 'just' war, that the use of force is justified (even if not legitimate) if you are protecting vital interests against an injustice, but world opinion in the 1950s was not persuaded of this. Nevertheless, British notions of international order and stability appeared to demand action – the 'quest for civilised behaviour'.[23] The perceptions amongst many people that Nasser had 'stolen' the canal, that his action was not a commendable example of national self-determination by a small state but a threat to international stability and security, cannot be overrated: 'I say . . . that we can have a situation in which the foe of genuine internationalism can be the modern nationalist, hysterical state, determined to act on its own irrespective of the interests of the rest of the world.'[24]

To many Nasser's actions were 'unjust' and it was not the correctness of the use of force which caused many of the divisions, but under whose auspices it was to be used. Gaitskell was as offended as Eden by the nationalisation and wished to bring the canal under international control, but force would have to be legitimised by the blessing of the United Nations.

Unfortunately for Eden's government, world opinion, particularly as expressed by the United Nations, did not share Britain's perception of Nasser's behaviour as a threat to international security, or as uncivilised, or Nasser himself as a nascent Hitler or Mussolini, and hence 'legitimise', through justification, British intervention.

Adequate Military Capabilities

The success of any military intervention ultimately rests upon the adequacy of military capabilities assigned to the task. 'Adequate military capabilities' not only refers to men and material but also to the planning and organisation of their use, though often one is dependent upon the other.

No contingency plan existed for the reoccupation of the Canal Zone, and Britain had withdrawn the last of 80,000 troops under the stipulations of the 1954 Treaty not long before the Canal Company was nationalised, though in 1956 there were still some British technicians on site at the base with over £40 million worth of stores.

The whole Suez crisis, however, revealed Britain's military weakness.

There was no base near enough to Egypt which could handle large ships and landing craft. The forces to hand in the region were not adequate for a large-scale invasion. The aircraft carrier at Malta and the two cruisers at Port Said were powerless if acting alone. There were political obstacles to using the 10th Armoured Division and the 10th Hussars in Libya against another Arab country. In Cyprus the Royal Horseguards and eight infantry battalions were all occupied in the campaign against the EOKA terrorists, while the three battalions of the Parachute regiment on the island had not done any recent training. There were no amphibious specialists on Cyprus and the transport aircraft available were only enough for a battalion. The inadequacy of ground and sea forces hampered the deployment of airborne forces, even if the necessary pilots, aircraft and trained paratroopers had been immediately available. Since the Second World War and the Arnhem experience it was deemed to be unwise to use paratroopers in a major action unless ground support was available within twenty-four hours. In 1956 British defence policy was simply not geared to a Suez-type expedition. Attention had been drawn to the desirability of a highly mobile strategic reserve in Defence White Papers in the early 1950s, notably in 1954, but by 1956 little had been achieved in that direction.[25] The year 1956 was the heyday of massive retaliation and British defence policy was organised around the concept of nuclear war or low-level colonial policing.

In addition to the paucity of appropriate British forces there was the problem of the Egyptian forces to be reckoned with, many of them British trained. In 1956 the Egyptian air force had 100 Migs, 100 medium tanks and 30 Ilyushin bombers, while Egyptian infantry were equipped with the new Czechoslovakian semi-automatic rifles. A quick operation – a *fait accompli* – was essential, but the Chiefs of Staff advised against an immediate military venture within forty-eight hours of the nationalisation as the military risks were too great. It was impossible to organise and transport an interventionary force to the canal quickly enough to forestall political pressures at home and abroad. The crisis dragged on for months before the interventionary forces were deemed to be ready and by that time much of the immediate justice of Britain's case had evaporated. The canal was functioning well under Egyptian control.

Finally, when the intervention took place, there was an overcommitment of the wrong sort of capabilities and as a result the political errors were compounded by the military inefficiencies. The intervention was slow and massive. It involved 80,000 troops, 150 warships including 7 aircraft carriers and 40 submarines, and 80 merchant ships carrying stores and 20,000 vehicles.[26] Port Said was bombed for six days before the invasion fleet, coming from a variety of ports such as Southampton, Algiers, Malta and Cyprus, positioned itself to land troops on 6 November.

Apparently Eisenhower was astounded by the incompetence of the operation. Bombing began on 31 October, then nothing happened. On 2 November there was the debate in the United Nations, on 3 November Egypt accepted the United Nations demand for a ceasefire, on 4 November Israel had achieved all its objectives, but still there was no invasion. On 5 November Anglo-French paratroopers eventually dropped on Egyptian territory. By this time a splinter group in the Conservative Party was voicing dissent, members of the Foreign Service had resigned, those still in the Foreign Office were dismayed, Gaitskell was calling on Eden to resign and the nation was anything but united in support of the government's resort to arms. On the morning of 6 November British and French forces waded ashore, ostensibly to separate combatants who had already stopped fighting each other. British forces performed well on the day and were less than twenty-five miles from Suez when Britain was obliged to agree to the United Nations call for a cease-fire at midnight of 6 November.

The military intervention, which had been so long in coming, contained absolutely no element of surprise and when it eventually occurred it was implemented so slowly and with such care that domestic and international opinion, public and official, was given ample opportunity to criticise and undermine the operation.

The United States

The Suez crisis and the intervention itself illustrate the necessity for a medium-rank power to achieve the approval and co-operation, public or tacit, of a superpower ally. In the Suez instance the opposition of the United States was one of the most decisive factors contributing to the failure of the Eden government's strategy. In the autumn of 1956 Britain found itself opposed not only by the Soviet Union, most of the Third World and most of the Commonwealth in its policy over the Suez Canal, but also by its major ally, the United States. The subsequent disaster revealed the fundamental weakness of Britain's claim to global power status: Britain had neither the military nor the economic resources to sustain such a position. Britain could no longer act independently of, or contrary to, the wishes of the United States, especially in high policy matters in the extra-European world. But why did the United States oppose the policy of its closest ally and, perhaps more important, how could the British government wage war without appreciating the United States perspective?

Unfortunately for Anthony Eden the Suez crisis occurred during a presidential election campaign. The United States presidential election was in November 1956 and Eisenhower wished to be seen as a 'man of peace'. The Geneva Summit had taken place the year before and it was an 'important moment in post-war relations because it signified that both super-powers were coming to understand that they might have certain interests in common, alongside many others that were conflictual, and that it might be worthwhile to search for ways to define and expand this area of communality'.[27] The 'Spirit of Geneva', based upon a joint United States and Soviet appreciation of the risks of nuclear war, was prevalent and Eisenhower, for genuine personal as well as electoral reasons, wished the mood to continue. On 31 July, five days after the nationalisation, Eisenhower wrote to Eden warning of the potentially hostile international opinion, including American, if military force was used: 'I have given you my own personal conviction, as well as that of my associates, as to the unwisdom of even contemplating the use of military force at this moment.' [28]

Eisenhower stressed the need to use all other peaceful means before considering the use of force. On 2 September he wrote a strong letter to Eden conveying opposition to force and the likely reaction in the United States to its use:

I must tell you frankly that American public opinion flatly rejects the thought of using force, particularly when it does not seem that every possible means of protecting our vital interests has been exhausted without result. Moreover, I gravely doubt we could here secure Congressional authority even for the lesser support measures for which you might have to look to us. I really do not see how a successful result could be achieved by forcible means. [29]

Eisenhower's opposition to force comes across loud and clear in such correspondence. The only explanation of the British misreading of the views of the Eisenhower administration is psychological. *In extremis*, how could their old ally possibly abandon them? Surely it was unthinkable? Macmillan, Eden's Chancellor, was one who strongly voiced such an opinion. However, such hopes were ill-founded and the contrived nature of the pretext for intervention did nothing to strengthen the British cause in Washington.

A very important consideration in American minds, ever aware of the global ideological contest with the Soviet Union, was to minimise the harmful effects of the Suez crisis on Western-Arab relations in the Middle East and not to antagonise the rest of the non-aligned Third World states. Prior to the period of vacillation between the Egyptian purchase of arms from the Soviet bloc and the withdrawal of aid for the Aswan Dam by the United States, Washington made strenuous efforts to be on good terms with Nasser. The United States had strongly encouraged the British to make concessions over the Suez Canal base in the 1953 negotiations and then offered Egypt military and economic assistance. Before the collapse of the Aswan Dam negotiations United States policy was to keep Soviet influence out of the Middle East, but by the autumn of 1956 United States policy had become one of damage-limitation:

The problem was now quite different: it was to avoid creating a situation in which the Soviet Union might expand further the considerable influence it had already achieved by deciding to give unequivocal support to the Arabs in the Palestine dispute and by arranging in 1956 to make arms available to Egypt ... the posture now assumed by the United States was linked closely with the administration's view with the requirements of defence, specifically, preventing the further expansion of Soviet influence in the Middle East.[30]

Another related factor in United States opposition to the British intervention was the antipathy within the United States foreign policy establishment, particularly felt by John Foster Dulles, towards colonialism, be it Soviet Russian or West European. Indeed, West European nineteenth-century-style colonial behaviour was seen by Washington as creating opportunities for the advancement of Soviet communism. The British determination to force the issue and to use military force to compel a minor, independent Third World state not only made the growth of communist influence more likely but fitted Dulles's model of colonialism. Management of the three-month crisis was not facilitated by the poor personal relationship between Eden and Dulles. Their temperaments and personal life-styles were very different, while professionally there had been disagreement over Indo-China in 1954, poor co-operation over the Suez base agreement of the same year, and Eden won a diplomatic coup in the London and Paris Agreement of 1954 and 1955 when Dulles appeared to have abandoned Europe in the wake of the failure of the European Defence Community.

The differences in the perspectives of the two men – Dulles saw Suez as hampering his efforts to contain communism, while Eden saw Nasser's behaviour as a threat not only to British interests but also to international order – becomes evident in Dulles's efforts between nationalisation and the Anglo-French intervention to dilute the crisis and stave off the use of military force. The instrument Dulles chose to achieve his desired ends was the proposal for a Suez Canal Users' Association (SCUA) – a club of maritime nations which would employ the pilots, collect dues and after deducting expenses pass on the profits to the Egyptian government. However, the success of SCUA was dependent upon two factors: first, member states would need to bring pressure to bear on flag ships to pay dues to the association and secondly, in the last resort SCUA would require the backing of military force. From 16 to 23 August twenty-two maritime nations met in conference in London, at Eden's invitation but at Dulles's suggestion. Eighteen of the participants agreed on the desirability of an international board, under United Nations auspices, to run the canal. This may have had the unfortunate effect of convincing the British government that eighteen states, including the United States, were essentially on its side. Despite Nasser's rejection of the SCUA idea on 9 September, Eden proposed and defended SCUA in the House of Commons on 12 September. That same day in the United States Dulles declared that SCUA nations should boycott the canal, but that the United States would not use force to support SCUA.

Eden felt betrayed but, under United States pressure, agreed to a second London conference thereby delaying any British appeal to the United

Nations. Dulles feared that the British would use the expected Soviet veto in the Security Council as a justification for military action; in addition, the United States was not too enthusiastic about using the United Nations to debate the Suez crisis in case, by association, the Panama Canal was dragged into the public discussion.[31] At the second London conference, beginning 19 September, little enthusiasm emerged in support of SCUA or the proposed boycott. Britain and France then decided to go to the Security Council as the prelude to the use of force but the United States did its best to keep the problem at as low a profile as possible and to spin out the proceedings.

As expected, on 13 October the Soviet Union vetoed SCUA at the United Nations. Eden was then even more determined to use force but, to a certain extent, Dulles's tactics of delay and postponement worked. As time passed the initial outrage in Britain subsided, the British press began to take a more rational view, the military and most of the Foreign Office became increasingly disenchanted with the prospect of force, the Labour Opposition became clearly against force and splits began to widen in Conservative Party ranks. Hence, when force was eventually used United States pressure was not pitted against a united, outraged nation but against an uncertain, isolated ruling clique with no solid unanimous base of public support and little, if any, international support.

Nevertheless, despite Eisenhower's warnings and Dulles's tactics Eden's government still presumed, in the last resort, that it had American support. At the worst, it was thought that the United States would remain an inactive spectator. Not only were the historical and cultural links of the 'Special Relationship' a basis for this misperception, but the United States was a NATO ally and, also, 'Eisenhower surely could not help but draw a parallel between the two canals, Suez and Panama. Americans might need the precedent of Musketeer;* this too should keep them quiet.'[32]

When the invasion took place United States opposition was the decisive factor in bringing about a ceasefire less than twenty-four hours after the first seaborne troops had waded ashore on the morning of 6 November. It is generally recognised that United States economic pressure obliged the British, to the chagrin of the French (dependent upon British logistics), to agree to a ceasefire with forces one-third of the way down the canal. The British Chiefs of Staff estimated that five more days were required to establish absolute control of the canal. On election day in the United States Humphrey, the Secretary of the Treasury, presented the British government with an ultimatum: ceasefire or

(i)   no more dollars forthcoming for oil purchases,
(ii) the United States would block an International Monetary Fund loan requested by Macmillan,
(iii) hopes for credit from the Export-Import bank would be seriously affected and

* Code-name for the Anglo-French invasion.

(iv)   no effort would be made to align United States central bankers behind
      sterling.[33]

In November 1956 Britain lost 15 per cent ($279 million) of its total gold
and dollar reserves: 'in 1956 the run on the pound and the American refusal
to authorise the £300 million the British had requested from the International Monetary Fund was the decisive reason why the Suez intervention
had to be halted'.[34]

For a short time Eden entertained the hope of using the Anglo-French
military presence as a bargaining counter but, with Nasser's refusal to allow
a United Nations peace-keeping force into Egypt until the Anglo-French
forces were out and with a further slump in the pound sterling in late
November and oil supplies running perilously short, Eden realised that any
thought of bargaining was unrealistic. Further perseverance would, in all
probability, have led to devaluation of the pound, severe petrol rationing,
repudiation of pledges to the sterling block, further uproar at the United
Nations, perhaps the break-up of the Commonwealth, greater opportunities
for the expansion of Soviet influence, more ministerial and civil service resignations and increased public divisiveness.

Realistic and Realisable Political Objective

A fundamental maxim of the use of force by one state against the other is, as
Clausewitz preached, to be aware of policy aims before war is waged: 'No war
should be commenced . . . without first seeking a reply to the question, What
is to be attained by and in the same?'[35] Furthermore, the first step should not
be taken 'without thinking what may be the last'.[36]

But what was Britain's political aim in the Suez intervention? If the military intervention had been successful and the canal had been captured, what
then? Allowed a free hand, Britain and France could have secured the canal
by 10 November but Britain and France had neither the power nor the
domestic will to reoccupy Egypt, depose Nasser and install a colonial administration. Nor were there any credible Egyptian puppet regimes waiting on
the sidelines. The conquest of Egypt and the removal of Nasser without a
popular replacement (and which government would have been popular if
supported in power by the British and the French?) would, in all likelihood,
have resulted in an immense, expensive, colonial peace-keeping headache of
the sort the British had abandoned with considerable relief in Palestine a few
years earlier.[37]

During the crisis Field Marshal Lord Montgomery, then deputy SACEUR,
asked to meet with Eden. When he inquired as to Eden's political objective
the reply was 'to knock Nasser off his perch'. Speaking of the occasion in the
House of Lords in 1962, Montgomery stated:

I said that if I were his military adviser – and I made it very clear that I was not – that object would not do. I should need to know what was the political object when Nasser had been knocked off his perch . . . because it was that which would determine how the operation was best carried out, what was the best disposition for our forces and so on. In my judgement, it was the uncertainty about the political object of our leaders which bedevilled the Suez operation from the beginning.[38]

Clear and identifiable political objectives were absent from the Suez intervention but future British attitudes to the use of force were greatly influenced by the Suez experience and in subsequent years great care was taken to relate force to political objectives:

The Suez operation was an aberrant and anachronistic use of force . . . and contrasts with other operations, such as the 'Confrontation' in Borneo from 1962–1966, where a minimum of force was used, in conjunction with positive and reasonable political aims, to achieve a political settlement.[39]

Some Results of the Suez Experience

The Suez experience had a number of related effects on British defence policy, some of which were short term and some of which were absorbed and continue to influence British defence policy to this day. One short-term effect was the severe disappointment in, and resultant distrust of, the United States as an ally. However, within a couple of years, facilitated by an extension of Anglo-American nuclear co-operation in 1958, the Macmillan administration successfully repaired the 'Special Relationship'. British defence policy planners were determined to ensure that, in future, British defence policy did not run counter to American planning but, nevertheless, the instance of abandonment by the United States at Suez did strengthen the resolve to pursue an independent nuclear deterrent programme. Despite Suez the 1957 Defence White Paper continued the fashionable total war perspective of the 1950s with its emphasis on high-technology rather than labour-intensive conventional forces, but by the late 1950s, for instance, the 1959 Defence White Paper, the limited war perspective was gaining increasing attention as the weaknesses of relying on nuclear weapons and high technology to implement all levels of policy came to be appreciated. However, the most important result of the Suez intervention was the determination, in future situations where military force could be required as an instrument of policy, not to make similar mistakes.

Notes: Chapter 2

1 Michael Carver, *War Since 1945* (London: Weidenfeld & Nicolson, 1980), introduction.
2 Hugh Thomas, *The Suez Affair* (London: Weidenfeld & Nicolson, 1967), p. 11.
3 See Richard E. Neustadt, *Alliance Politics* (New York and London: Columbia University Press, 1970), p. 10.
4 For a description of the difficulties involved in the Tripartite agreement, see Dwight D. Eisenhower, *Waging Peace* (London: Heinemann, 1966), p. 24.
5 See David Childs, *Britain since 1945* (London: Ernest Benn, 1979), p. 85.
6 Eisenhower, op. cit., p. 33.
7 See F. S. Northedge, *Descent from Power* (London: Allen & Unwin, 1974), p. 129.
8 Neustadt, op. cit., p. 12.
9 See *Defence: Outline of Future Policy*, Cmnd 124 (London: HMSO, 1957).
10 Northedge, op. cit., p. 113.
11 ibid., p. 125.
12 Thomas, op. cit., p. 64.
13 For 'confirmation' of collusion, see Antony Nutting, *No End of a Lesson: The Story of Suez* (London: Constable, 1967), p. 104; Moshe Dayan, *Story of My Life* (London: Weidenfeld & Nicolson, 1976), pp. 179 and 192–3; and David Carlton, *Anthony Eden* (London: Allen Lane, 1981), pp. 430–41.
14 For a recent analysis of the evidence and the literature, see Geoffrey Warner, ' "Collusion" and the Suez crisis of 1956', *International Affairs*, vol. 55, no. 2 (1979), pp. 226–39.
15 See Robert Skidelsky, 'Lessons of Suez', in V. Bogdanor and R. Skidelsky (eds), *The Age of Affluence 1951–1964* (London: Macmillan, 1970), p. 176.
16 See Townsend Hoopes, *The Devil and John Foster Dulles* (London: Andre Deutsch, 1974), p. 347, and Bernard Levin, 'Lord Mountbatten and the Suez affair: how the truth was nearly suppressed', *The Times*, 5 November 1980, p. 14.
17 See Harold Macmillan, *Riding the Storm* (London: Macmillan, 1971), pp. 99–100.
18 See Northedge, op. cit., pp. 130–1.
19 Thomas, op. cit., p. 133.
20 R. Osgood and R. Tucker, *Force, Order and Justice* (Baltimore, Md: Johns Hopkins University Press, 1967), p. 228.
21 See Thomas, op. cit., p. 39. For a detailed legal appreciation of the Suez affair see Robert Bowie, *Suez 1956* (London: Oxford University Press, 1974).
22 Quincy Wright, *A Study of War* (Chicago and London: University of Chicago Press, 1969), p. 16.
23 Skidelsky, op. cit., p. 173.
24 Herbert Morrison (Labour), *Hansard*, vol. 531, col. 760, quoted in Skidelsky, op. cit., p. 175.
25 See John Baylis, 'British defence policy', in John Baylis *et al.*, *Contemporary Strategy, Theories and Policies* (London: Croom Helm, 1975), p. 273.
26 See Joseph Frankel, *British Foreign Policy 1945–1973* (London: Oxford University Press, 1975), p. 85.
27 A. W. De Porte, *Europe Between the Superpowers* (New Haven, Conn., and London: Yale University Press, 1979), p. 174.
28 Eisenhower, op. cit., p. 664.
29 ibid., p. 667.
30 Robert C. Good, 'The United States and the colonial debate', in Arnold Wolfers (ed.), *Alliance Policy in the Cold War* (Baltimore, Md: Johns Hopkins University Press, 1959), pp. 256–7.
31 See Lincoln P. Bloomfield, *The United Nations and United States Foreign Policy* (London: University of London Press, 1969), p. 168.
32 Neustadt, op. cit., pp. 21–2.
33 ibid., p. 26.

34　Frankel, op. cit., p. 87.
35　Karl von Clausewitz, *On War* (English edition, revised by Colonel F. N. Maude, 1908), bk III, p. 79, quoted in J. F. C. Fuller, *The Conduct of War* (London: Eyre Methuen, 1972), p. 66.
36　ibid., p. 87, quoted in Fuller, op. cit., p. 66.
37　See Klaus Knorr, *On the Uses of Military Power in the Nuclear Age* (Princeton, NJ: Princeton University Press, 1966), p. 77.
38　Quoted in Thomas, op. cit., p. 90.
39　Peter Nailor, 'Defence policy and foreign policy', in R. Boardman and A. J. Groom (eds), *The Management of Britain's External Relations* (London: Macmillan, 1973), p. 230.

3 *The Intervention Environment: 1956–75*

In the decade following the Suez crisis, and despite the weakness in national power painfully revealed by the Suez affair, British governments of both the major political parties attempted to perpetuate Britain's traditional global political and military role. It was in the ten years following Suez that a number of successful British military interventions (which will be examined in detail in Chapter 4) took place – often being used as evidence to support Britain's continuing role outside the NATO area. However, by the mid-1960s two major, tangible, interrelated constraints began to be acutely felt in British defence policy – constraints which eventually brought about the abandonment of the interventionary role. The constraints in question were (i) economic and (ii) operational, but not directly political. The will to maintain an oceanic role and procure the appropriate capabilities was much in evidence until the late 1960s. The constraints in question had been clearly evident since the early postwar years but, although some political retrenchments had taken place, for example, the abandonment of the Palestine Mandate, commitments continued to stretch capabilities severely. In the 1980s the political will to project military power outside Europe may have revived, but the constraints experienced in the 1960s are even more in evidence. Britain may no longer claim to be a global power, but in any attempt to use military force for political purposes beyond the North Atlantic problems and questions arise similar to those encountered in the post-Suez period under examination in this chapter. To appreciate the intervention/non-intervention debate of these years it is necessary to examine the politico-strategic environment in which Britain found itself and the constraints which proved insurmountable.

Britain and the International System

In the late 1950s, despite the independence of India a decade earlier and the gathering pace of decolonisation, and notwithstanding the catastrophe of Suez, Britain still perceived itself to be a world power. Although the Empire was slowly but surely disappearing Britain's continuing involvement in global international affairs was perceived to be required for two major related reasons, both of which were articulated during the Suez crisis but nevertheless lost some of their appeal to much of the British foreign policy establishment because of it. First, the communist threat had to be contained, and in that task the United States required British moral and material support; secondly, a stable international system, with particular reference to the newly independent states, often former British colonies, was seen to be in the West's, and especially Britain's, diplomatic and economic interests.[1] In the latter respect Britain not only felt some sense of residual post-imperial responsibility (particularly so among Labour politicians towards the New Commonwealth post-1947), but because of its self-perceived liberal and beneficent imperial past, considered itself to be uniquely qualified for the job: 'The politicians ... suffered from a hangover of a Gladstonian view that Britain had somehow a more moral idea of world order than other more selfish powers, and therefore had both a greater duty and greater right to act as a world policeman.'[2] Even a decade after Suez Britain still pursued a role in maintaining international, not merely European, security: '[Britain] shares with other countries a general interest in seeing peace maintained, so far as possible, throughout the world. It is this interest above all which justifies our military presence outside Europe.'[3]

Outside West Europe nearly all British commitments were the residue of Empire. By the late 1950s and early 1960s withdrawal from Empire was in full swing and, for those countries that wished, defence agreements and military support were proffered. Some chose not to accept, or abrogated treaties soon after independence (e.g. Nigeria and Sierra Leone), not wishing to be associated with Western containment strategy or to be vulnerable to accusations of neo-colonialism;[4] while other newly independent states were only too happy to accept, and benefit from, security arrangements with Britain. British governments not only felt responsible, but displayed no little pride at being able to contribute to order and security when requested:

> We have responded five times in the past two weeks to appeals from Commonwealth partners whose life and independence have been threatened. In Malaysia we are there to prevent a Commonwealth country being dismembered by subversion and force. In Cyprus we are there to prevent a very unhappy people suffering from civil war in the island and to prevent Greece and Turkey from being drawn into the war. In Kenya, Uganda and Tanganyika we are there in response to requests from their governments to prevent illegal takeovers by mutinous elements who would overthrow the elected Governments who are only a few months, or indeed, a few weeks old ... I hope therefore, that the Commonwealth countries understand that when the chips are down, the Commonwealth can rely on Britain.[5]

Global influence and status had a similar attraction for the Labour Party when in office, despite the tortuous, internecine debates over defence policy while in Opposition. Coming to office in October 1964, Harold Wilson said, 'We are a world power and a world influence or we are nothing'.[6] Ironically, at this period, British possession of a nuclear deterrent was seen by both major political parties, Conservative in and out of office, and Labour once in office, not only as underwriting Britain's great-power status, but as a weapons system which, first, allowed defence savings over the long run and hence released resources for conventional forces for east of Suez operations and, secondly, had potential relevance for a peace-keeping role outside NATO. Labour government thinking in 1965 was that, *inter alia*, the Polaris deterrent could be used to protect India from a massive Chinese conventional attack while, it was hoped, India could be dissuaded from procuring its own nuclear deterrent.[7]

In the years between Suez and the success of the Labour Party at the polls in 1964 the Conservative governments of Macmillan and Douglas-Home were, naturally, convinced of Britain's future role. The rapid Anglo-US rapprochement after Suez encouraged the Conservatives in that belief, and although attempts were made to rationalise defence policy in terms of defence procurement and organisation, such as the phasing out of National Service from 1957, little attempt was made to rationalise commitments. The major threats to international security were perceived to lie outside Europe, and Britain had a unique role to play. As Harold Macmillan described it: 'We have, of course, to make a contribution, and we are making it loyally to the NATO forces, but we have obligations also in many other parts of the world, and the defence of the free world, and indeed the survival of the free world, is assisted by our efforts in some of these more distant areas.'[8]

In the context of such a policy as described above, and despite possession of nuclear weapons, there was recognition in the Conservative government, from 1954 onwards,[9] and also by some in the Labour Party such as Emanuel Shinwell, of the increasing need for improved limited war capabilities if such a role was to be pursued effectively. Following the Berlin and Cuban crises Europe was perceived to be quiescent, secure in an arms balance favourable to the West, while east of Suez was identified as the area of greatest potential conflict. The Chiefs of Staff Paper of January 1962 laid emphasis on the need to maintain limited war capabilities for use east of Suez. The recent Kuwait operation appeared to vindicate such a view. Although lip-service had been paid to the need for a mobile strategic reserve since the mid-1950s, the total war theme had permeated British defence policy until the early 1960s. The only service to have attempted to equip itself seriously for limited war had been the Royal Navy, perhaps less through foresight than in the search for a role. However, any effective interventionary limited war force would require transport aircraft, and also aircraft carriers as the hub of seaborne task forces. After 1962 moves were made to upgrade these components of British power projection.[10]

In opposition the Labour Party was suggesting that the east of Suez role would cause rather than deter trouble. However, following Gaitskell's death and with the election of Wilson in 1963 to the party leadership, the Shadow Front Bench chose to re-examine Britain's role. As a result official Labour

Party policy was changed, and it was held, though by no means unanimously throughout the Parliamentary Party, that Britain had a valid and unique role east of Suez.

Such Labour support was, perhaps, partly a function of Wilson's reluctance to contemplate entry to the EEC. Nevertheless, for a number of reasons there was by 1964 bipartisan political support for Britain's post-imperial world role and concomitant commitments.

The Labour government's first defence statement clearly reveals that, while aware of the need for defence expenditure retrenchment, east of Suez was identified as the danger area, and Britain had a distinct role to fulfil in that region:

> It is therefore pointless to tie up resources against the risks of a prolonged war in Europe following the nuclear exchange ... The British contribution is paramount in many areas East of Suez ... Our presence in these bases, our Commonwealth ties, and the mobility of our forces, permit us to make a contribution toward peacekeeping in vast areas of the world where no other country is able to assume the same responsibility.[11]

Reed and Williams describe the prevalent feeling in the Labour Party about Britain's global role at the time of accession to power in 1964 thus:

> The role of providing a fire brigade for the world's trouble spots was one of immense appeal for the Labour Government of Harold Wilson ... Buying time for small nations so that they could build up their economies and forces to a point where they could look after themselves appealed to the 'internationalists'.[12]

Though Harold Wilson may have entertained notions of a much higher diplomatic role for Britain under his premiership, as an arbiter between the United States and Soviet Union, the Labour government in general, and Denis Healey, the Defence Secretary, in particular, saw Britain's role outside Europe as essentially a stability-maintenance and a stability-inducing role.[13] Though objecting to Labour's cuts in projected defence expenditure, such as the cancellation of the fifth Polaris submarine and the TSR2 aircraft, the Conservative Party was in full agreement with continuing the extra-North Atlantic role.

In addition, there was steady and public Commonwealth support for the maintenance of a major British presence east of Suez, especially from Australia, New Zealand, Malaysia and India. Similarly, the United States welcomed the British presence. Robert McNamara, Defence Secretary for all of the Kennedy and most of the Johnson administrations, stated that 'British troops east of Suez were more valuable man for man, than those on the Rhine'.[14] Unlike the situation in the nineteenth and early twentieth centuries, Britain no longer possessed the economic power to pose a serious challenge to United States influence in the developing world, but its military and moral support in preserving international order was welcome: 'the USA which in the past had distrusted Britain's imperial positions and intentions switched in the sixties to a policy of urging Britain to stay and share the burdens of peace-keeping and anti-communist containment'.[15]

However, although the *will* to project military power was present, ever-pressing financial considerations raised large questions as to Britain's capabilities to fulfil such a role effectively. Within eighteen months of Labour coming to office signs of retrenchment overseas and a diminution of the much-supported role were evident, with the announcement, in the 1966 Defence White Paper, of the policy of withdrawal from Aden by 1968 and no further overseas interventions without the support of allies. Worsening balance of payments, and the perception that overseas defence spending was a major contributing factor, meant that the writing was on the wall for Britain's defence role outside NATO. The inevitability and rapidity of the process was accelerated by the devaluation of sterling in November 1967. With the appreciation of the constraints official attitudes changed and an *ex post facto* rationalisation of the predicament took place. Britain was now a 'European' power. British forces, suffering severe overstretch east of Suez, now had a role in Europe, and the threat east of Suez had subsided while the threat in the NATO area was rising. This was all probably true, but ironically these new directions in British defence policy, more efficacious in cost-benefit terms than the old policies, resulted from the failure to overcome constraints against which successive British governments had been battling since 1945, rather than the coincidental conversion of Harold Wilson to an enthusiasm for the EEC in 1967.[16]

However, in some ways the strength of the constraints had a positive effect:

> Available resources define the limits of policy choice, but it is when a constraint 'bites' that these boundaries are illuminated sharply. Queries then arise about purposes or objectives which may have been taken for granted. It becomes impossible to avoid asking whether a particular use of resources confers benefits commensurate with the costs in terms of alternative values forgone. These choices are *not* continuously in the forefront of attention.[17]

The perceived necessity for defence retrenchment also coincided with the development of East—West détente and the beginning of the 'era of negotiations'. SALT opened at Helsinki in November 1969 and at the same time the Brandt administration began its Ostpolitik. NATO was seen as a vehicle to influence the United States, and as an instrument to prevent the United States and other Alliance members settling issues vital to European security over the heads of their European partners. Britain, as a European nuclear and conventional military power, with an obvious security interest in SALT,

Ostpolitik and the future of Berlin, began to be a strong advocate of a 'European defence identity'.[18] In London's eyes détente was a problematical diplomatic process, containing many challenges but also opportunities. To maximise the opportunities NATO had to appear strong and cohesive, and British influence had a distinct role to play.

The British withdrawal from the defence role outside NATO and cuts in defence expenditure were not unpopular. Ephemeral post-imperial tasks in faraway places did not arouse public enthusiasm, especially as hard domestic concerns began to compete with defence expenditure for attention. Indeed, in the postwar era, defence policy has rarely been a high profile public issue:

> Such evidence as there is confirms that public opinion on defence is generally one of apathy. In the seven elections between 1945 and 1970 defence was only an issue in 1951 at the time of the Korean War.[19]

In a 1967 Gallup Poll 70 per cent interviewed considered that priority should be given to education over defence.[20] The public opinion which affects and guides defence policy, however, is the opinion of the 'interested public', that is, interested professionals such as journalists, academics, politicians, senior civil servants and senior military officers. In democracies public opinion at large tends to become involved in foreign policy only occasionally and then usually in a negative fashion, that is, when a policy is being pursued which it finds too costly in all sorts of ways and wishes to be stopped; for example, the reaction to the Vietnam War in the United States.

The 1966 Defence White Paper indicated that financial constraints would oblige Britain to impose some limitations on global commitments. The move towards Europe was made explicit in the Supplementary Statement on Defence of July 1967, published during Britain's negotiations to join the EEC:

> The security of Britain still depends above all on the prevention of war in Europe. We, therefore, regard it as essential to maintain both the military efficiency and political solidarity of the North Atlantic Treaty Organisation. For this purpose, we must continue to make a substantial contribution to NATO's forces in order to play a part in the defence of Europe and to maintain the necessary balance within the Western Alliance. This contribution will become even more important as we develop closer political and economic ties between Britain and her European neighbours.[21]

Before leaving office in 1970 Denis Healey laid the groundwork for the 'Eurogroup' – an informal committee of interested NATO European defence ministers – and the subsequent emergence of a strong European defence identity. In the NATO context Britain perceived itself, once again, as somewhat special – a claim justified, in British eyes, by the American connection, nuclear status and a spread of military forces, on land, sea and air, along the whole length of NATO's front with the Warsaw Pact: 'if Britain was laying down a "world role" East of Suez, it was hoping to fill a "central role" among the European allies of NATO'.[22]

The Heath administration came to power in June 1970, enthusiastically pro-European, but with the traditional Conservative interest in global affairs.[23] The Heath government was inclined to maintain some presence east of Suez, one result of which was the Five Power Defence Agreement with Australia, New Zealand, Malaysia and Singapore, but there was to be no return to pre-devaluation days. The British became enthusiastic participants in the European Defence Improvement Programme, whereby the Eurogroup powers increased their defence expenditures as an effort to show willing in sharing more of the NATO security burden with the United States. The return of the Labour Party to power in 1974 confirmed the Eurocentrism of British defence policy, and the inevitable phasing-out of any significant military presence east of Suez other than colonial policing obligations such as Hong Kong, or small contingents fulfilling technical duties, such as on the island of Gan. The decisions in the 1975 Defence Review[24] to scrap attack aircraft carriers and abandon the Simonstown base in South Africa were indicative of this policy, and seemed to suggest it was irreversible.

Defence policy pronouncements of the Conservative government of Margaret Thatcher, suggesting that some capabilities to facilitate the projection of military force outside the North Atlantic area should be procured, indicate a revival of the propensity, in some quarters, to undertake again a serious extra-North Atlantic military role after a decade of concentration on Europe. Once again the Indian Ocean littoral and hinterlands are perceived as the area of greatest potential conflict and instability, posing a considerable threat to Britain and the West's trade and sources of vital raw materials.

However, the intervention environment of the 1980s will be very different from that of the 1960s. In the 1960s not only was there a strong political will and bipartisan political support but the environment in which forces operated was much less hostile than can be expected in the 1980s in that indigenous forces opposing British intervention were not so well armed, and there was no significant possibility of encountering Soviet forces or Soviet-sponsored forces. Nevertheless, despite such 'environmental' advantages, few of which will be repeated in the 1980s, the major constraints encountered by Britain could not be overcome. These constraints are still present, and are even more inhibitive of the long-range projection of military force by medium-rank powers than they were twenty years ago. Hence an appreciation of the effect of these constraints – economic and operational – on British policy in the 1960s is worthwhile.

Economic Constraints

In the interwar years defence expenditure was an issue of debate but not a pressing problem, at least until the late 1930s when rapid rearmament began to threaten national bankruptcy.[25] For most of the interwar period British defence focused on two major concerns: (i) defence of the home islands and (ii) defence of the Empire, necessitating the maintenance of the fleet and overseas bases. It was the latter function which was the most expensive but, none the less, on average only 3 per cent of the GNP was devoted to defence, and the total manpower in the three services was little above 300,000. Britain's global power was based upon its position as a leading, though declining, economic power, on the Royal Navy's control of lines of communication to the Empire and on the military resources of Empire, notably the Indian army. Until the years of rearmament European security concerns were viewed as secondary, and in the capable hands of the deterrent power of the RAF bomber fleets. The Second World War, of course, drastically changed this state of affairs. By 1946 the British defence estimates were at £1.7 billion,[26] and in 1948, three years into demobilisation, there were still 940,000[27] uniformed personnel in the British forces. The years after 1945 witnessed a permanent military force on the continent of Europe, a rundown economy and massive depletion of foreign investments caused by the cost of the war, and the erosion of the power provided by Empire. The year 1947 was the beginning of the decline of Empire with the independence of India. A formal commitment was removed (although a residual one remained, especially in the eyes of the Labour Party) but, most important for British defence policy, Britain lost a vast reservoir of manpower. Britain's capacity to maintain and protect the colonies, project military power, and provide political leadership to the Commonwealth was, to a great extent, derived from Empire itself. However, decolonisation did not mean that commitments disappeared, merely the resources. Defence agreements with the new states perpetuated the commitments, on top of which could be added NATO and later CENTO burdens.

The perpetuation and enlargement of defence commitments was taking place simultaneously with the development of an awareness that the revitalisation of the British economy was a necessity, but the Cold War was at its height, and the Korean War intensified concern over Western security. At a time when the British economy was desperately needing new investment the Attlee administration of 1950 felt obliged to devote 10 per cent of the GNP to the defence budget. There was a need for a compromise between domestic demands and an adequate defence posture. One was impossible without the other, but during the Korean period massive export and domestic recovery potential was being lost to the armaments industry. Ironically the economy could not bear the attempt at massive rearmament during the Korean War, and the economic problems raised were, perhaps, the major reason for the return of Churchill to power in 1951, with the Conservatives subsequently cutting the defence budget from the heights it had reached in 1950 and 1951.

The Suez crisis of 1956 emphasised Britain's economic weakness, and the experience contributed, for a short spell, to plans for even more unbalanced forces. 'Why maintain expensive conventional forces when they could not win at Suez?' was the question asked, rather than 'how do we improve our limited war and interventionary forces to cope successfully with Suez-type operations?' Hence, in the so-called revolutionary Defence White Paper of Duncan Sandys[28] in 1957, money was going to be saved but great-power influence maintained through technology replacing manpower, National Service being phased out and the continued development of Britain's nuclear deterrent. A central reserve of long-range air transport and seaborne forces would handle local conflicts, but little discussion was devoted to the planning, organisation and role of such a force. Commitments, however, were not reduced commensurate with the planned arms base. More widely unbalanced forces were expected to service an unchanged spread of commitments: 'the supposedly radical defence policy of 1957 must therefore be regarded as essentially traditional. It was yet another attempt to continue the whole familiar gamut of British military roles within increasing economic constraints.'[29] But, only months after the 1957 Defence White Paper was published, the new Chancellor of the Exchequer was calling for further reductions in the defence budget. The Sandys strategy had not neutralised the economic constraints.

One of the major burdens on the defence budget at this time was the increasing cost of advanced military technology. As manpower was reduced the savings were more than absorbed by the cost of new weaponry. Aircraft carriers costing £3 million in the 1930s were costing £30 million by the 1960s, and by 1960 the cost of army equipment had increased fourfold in twenty years. Nevertheless, in the closing years of the 1959–64 Conservative government, when a chronic balance-of-payments deficit and the need for investment in the domestic economy clashed with defence expenditure, the government persisted with attempts to maintain the traditional British military role.

When the Wilson government assumed office defence expenditure was running at £1·963 billion, which was about a quarter of the whole government budget, and 5·9 per cent of the GNP. It was reckoned that the east of Suez military role was absorbing about a quarter of the defence budget,[30] which was roughly the equivalent of the 1964 balance-of-payments deficit of £747 million. Consequently there was a tendency to look to defence cuts as the answer to the country's economic problems, and a 'value for money' approach was adopted, with an attempt to reduce defence spending to £2,000 million at 1964 prices by 1970. Indicative of this was the introduction into the Ministry of Defence, which took its cue from the 1961 Plowden Report on the Control of Public Expenditure, of new management and analysis techniques in order to facilitate a more rational view of defence. The concepts and tools of programme budgeting, functional costing and cost-effectiveness had been introduced successfully into the Pentagon by Robert McNamara. This process became known as the planning, programming, budgeting system:

The basic idea behind programme budgeting was to make decisions after rational and explicit reasoning. It involves planning, defining objectives, breaking down a programme into its constituent parts, then working out what each would cost and finally estimating its efficiency.[31]

Ideally, with goals firmly fixed, departmental spending would be co-ordinated (in Britain by the Public Expenditure Survey Committee – a procedural innovation of the Wilson government) and planned not only over the forthcoming year, but over a programme of a number of years, usually four. In defence it was hoped that functional costing, that is, budgets for air mobility, research and development, European theatre ground forces, and so on, rather than for the RAF or the RN, would lend some stability and rationality to defence planning, and minimise the risk of haphazard defence cuts. Defence functions rather than service budgets would be viewed in the light of other governmental functions, and some measure of cost-effectiveness taken, though it is always problematic to measure the 'efficiency' of defence.[32]

Economic constraints and the search for 'value for money' resulted in a number of weapon programmes being cancelled, most notably the TSR2 and the projected fifth Polaris submarine. Indeed, the record of the British government in this regard, throughout the 1950s and the first half of the 1960s, is lamentable. In the aircraft industry, which suffered most of the cancellations, Britain invested over £300 million between 1952 and 1965 in aircraft projects which were eventually cancelled. This represented 20 per cent of the total research and development in aerospace, but the implications were not merely financial as precious time was lost in developing and producing replacements. In the mid-1960s it was reckoned that the defence effort required some 1,400,000 of the nation's manpower, about one-fifth of the scientists and engineers and about two-fifths of the total expenditure on research and development.[33]

By 1964 the east of Suez role was perceived as the main drain on resources, particularly as the Federal Republic of Germany was bearing an increasing share of the foreign exchange costs of the British Army of the Rhine. In 1967 overseas spending by the British government reached £446 million, with defence accounting for over two-thirds. An indication of the savings possible was shown by the reduction of foreign exchange costs by £8 million when 10,000 servicemen returned to Britain following the end of the Confrontation between Malaysia and Indonesia and the signing of the Bangkok Agreement in 1966. In 1966 the annual budgetary cost of maintaining all British forces east of Suez was £330 million, with personnel and equipment costing £115 million and £147 million respectively of the total,[34] and escalating all the time as the forces became 'professionalised', and new military equipment became more advanced technologically and hence much more expensive. British military manpower, at its lowest level since 1945 at just over 420,000, was perilously overstretched, and it was openly admitted that a major conflict east of Suez would require the removal of troops from

BAOR. Britain could not afford large forces beyond the North Atlantic, particularly with increasing emphasis being given to 'labour-intensive' limited war operations after 1962. The costs of personnel, equipment and bases were beyond Britain's resources, especially as equipment and training for Britain's east of Suez forces was different from that required for Britain's NATO forces.

None the less, the decision to undertake a major withdrawal was deferred as long as possible. In 1966, in Canberra, Denis Healey stated that 'The [Defence] Review has been concerned not with the next few years but ... with the years from 1970 to 1980, and to some extent from 1980 to 1990, and I think the most important conclusion I am able to communicate to you is that we do intend to remain, in the military sense, a world power'.[35] Similar sentiments were expressed in the February 1967 Defence White Paper where a resolve to maintain a presence east of Suez 'in which British forces can help create an environment in which local governments are able to establish the political and economic basis for peace and stability' was articulated.[36]

But seemingly perpetual balance-of-payments crises and mounting pressure from sections of the Parliamentary Labour Party[37] resulted in the Supplementary Defence White Paper of July 1967 which laid down a timetable of withdrawal for forces in Singapore and Malaysia by the mid-1970s, the phasing-out of an aircraft carrier presence, and the halving of forces in the Persian Gulf. The necessity to reduce overseas expenditure was explicitly cited as the reason for the retrenchments, but Britain would attempt to honour its commitments by a maritime presence and a capacity to intervene by air. Devaluation in November 1967 brought these short-lived good intentions to an end. The February 1968 Defence White Paper decreed wide-ranging defence cuts resulting in withdrawal from Malaysia, Singapore and the Persian Gulf by the end of 1971. Long-range air strike capability in the form of an order with the United States for 75 F111 aircraft was cancelled, and the concept of a permanent maritime presence became redundant. British military power for extra-North Atlantic purposes was to reside in a vague 'general capability' derived from forces maintained for NATO roles. As the 1968 Defence White Paper stated, 'Britain's defence effort will in future be concentrated in Europe and the North Atlantic area'.[38]

This turnabout in British defence strategy, which introduced more than a decade of disenchantment with any military role outside NATO, was due primarily to economic constraints. There was always a section in the Parliamentary Labour Party, contained until 1967, which opposed the east of Suez strategy, but its influence and the strength of its argument, which reached into the heart of the Cabinet, became irresistible with devaluation.[39]

Operational Constraints

The economic constraints on the long-range projection of British military force contributed considerably to the operational problems encountered in the period under discussion. One of the chief operational constraints was manpower overstretch. In any emergency British forces were stretched, often dangerously, and the progressive manpower cuts of the post-1957 years only aggravated the situation. Between 1960 and 1970 the British army fell by over 160,000 men, the RAF by 50,000 and the RN by 13,000, but until the 1970s there was little significant change in the global spread of British forces. In 1960 British troops were stationed in the Bahamas, Jamaica, British Honduras, British Guiana, Libya, Gibraltar, Malta, Cyprus, East Africa, Aden, the Persian Gulf, Singapore, Malaya and Hong Kong.[40] By 1970 British forces were still in the Caribbean, the Persian Gulf, South-East Asia, Hong Kong and the Mediterranean, as well as fulfilling NATO duties in Europe and providing aid to the civil power in Northern Ireland.

The concept of an airborne strategic reserve was favoured, for a spell, as a solution to many problems, and between the late 1950s and mid-1960s a vast increase in transport capabilities took place. Up until the late 1950s RAF Transport Command was viewed very much as a poor relation to Bomber and Fighter Commands. One can identify two reasons for the subsequent change of outlook. First, transport, in an era when there were growing doubts over the viability of bomber forces, provided a new role and some means of maintaining aircraft numbers at a respectable level. This new role was accepted and defended by the RAF throughout the 1960s:

> Military reaction must be capable of immediate response in the required strength which would be impossible, in view of the world wide stage, unless it had a very high degree of mobility and speed. Nothing, indeed, short of air movement can hope to meet emergencies in time in the modern age.[41]

Secondly, though by no means less important, developing transport capabilities was seen as a way of partially resolving the capabilities/commitments inconsistencies in British defence policy. A mobile strategy would allow skeleton forces east of Suez, while air transportable forces would be held in reserve in the UK and West Germany. The year 1959 saw the Air Ministry decide to reactivate No. 38 Group, previously disbanded in 1951, whose function was to co-ordinate land–air operations. It was to develop into a self-contained force equipped with a variety of transport aircraft, helicopters and, in the second half of the 1960s, fighter and ground attack squadrons.

But the concept of an air-mobile strategic reserve to operate over continental distances was discovered to have considerable weaknesses. Owing to the political problem of over-flying rights there could never be any guarantee that countries on the most direct route to any crisis spot would be sympathetic towards the purposes of any British intervention in their part of the world, or that countries over which British aircraft had to pass would not simply be ideologically hostile to Britain. Roundabout air routes could remove elements of surprise, would necessitate politically sensitive and economically expensive staging posts and would most certainly complicate the logistics problem of supply and reinforcement. Furthermore, special light scales equipment is required for air travel, but such equipment must be able to sustain and protect the airborne forces if they are obliged to operate in a hostile environment for some period of time. The type of aircraft to be procured for long-range interventions is also a problem. Long-range heavy-load-bearing aircraft are not only very expensive and require long runways to land, but need considerable maintenance, especially in hot climates. In the 1960s the RAF found that the mechanics of the Beverly heavy-load aircraft did not always react well to hot climates, that there were often problems of serviceability and, on occasions, it was necessary to reduce total loads. There is also the problem of fighter support if operating in a hostile environment and, in recent years, the need for protection from surface-to-air missiles, no longer the prerogative of the sophisticated armies of developed countries. Anyway, it was realised that it was impossible to move all equipment by air, so depots for heavy equipment had to be established at focal points such as Singapore. Air mobility was no substitute for a permanent, on-the-ground, large-scale presence: 'it became apparent that the scale of the East of Suez role and the inevitable restrictions in the development of a massive air transport fleet . . . meant that air mobility could only be a partial solution to Britain's problems'.[42]

To make up for shortfalls of equipment and personnel outside Europe forces were, on occasions, withdrawn from NATO roles but the scale of such transfers was limited by the obvious disapproval of the European allies. Before 1968 matters were further complicated by United States encouragement of Britain to continue its extra-North Atlantic role. However, after 1968, when the economic constraints acting on Britain were painfully apparent, and with Nixon rather than Johnson in the White House, the United States began to support Britain in the EEC rather than Britain east of Suez.

Illustrative of the problem of maintaining an operational presence outside Europe in this period, and of the attempts to follow the most cost-effective route only to be sabotaged by devaluation, was the CVA-01 (aircraft carrier) versus F111/island base debate of 1964–6. Against a background of ever-increasing economic constraints, the RAF found itself coming into sharp and sometimes acrimonious competition with the RN for the limited resources to be spent east of Suez. The culmination of this competition was the F111/CVA-01 debate. In 1960 Air Chief Marshal Sir Edmund Huddleston, then Vice Chief of Air Staff, suggested the development of Indian Ocean island bases for the purpose of facilitating refuelling of long-range aircraft, thereby overcoming the air barrier arguments to air mobility. Utilising these island bases for strike/reconnaissance aircraft developed into an alternative to expensive aircraft carriers. Some islands such as Gan and Masirah had already been developed by 1965, and others such as Aldabra and Prince Edward Island were surveyed and considered.

By July 1964, with the Anglo-US survey of Diego Garcia and Aldabra as prospective sites, complementing British bases at Aden and Singapore, the challenge to the RN became clear and the debate intensified. United States Secretary for Defence Robert McNamara, enthusiastic for the Indian Ocean to remain a British sphere of influence, contributed Pentagon support to the island base scheme.

The hard lines drawn by the '£2,000m.' defence budget created a distinct division of opinion between the RAF and RN by 1965. The RN carriers and the RAF's F111s, which could well have complemented each other in an east of Suez peace-keeping role, could not both be contained within the defence budget.

Late 1965 saw the RN make a bid to place an order for a new aircraft carrier – the CVA-01. No approach was made for CVA-02, as the Admiralty saw this as a tactical error until CVA-01 was on the slipway. However, if Britain was going to rely on carriers, the Ministry of Defence was well aware that a minimum of three new carriers would be required. At the same time the RAF asked for seventy-five F111s.

Although the F111 case stood independently, the RAF also argued that such a force, together with certain other aircraft, working from island bases and in conjunction with the Australians, could well replace the aircraft carrier system in the Indian Ocean. Because the construction period for CVA-01 was eight years, a decision was necessary in 1966. Adopting a quantitative approach, as well as arguing the operational advantages of the island base scheme,[43] the RAF had the upper hand.

If the operational environment is too hostile for strike aircraft, of what additional advantage is an aircraft carrier? If an aircraft carrier is destroyed there is a great loss of prestige, manpower and investment. While carrier forces can be on the spot, 'show the flag' and conduct low-intensity operations, more than one force would be required, and more than 25 per cent of an aircraft carrier's life is spent in refit. It would take a carrier force twenty-four hours to cover 800 miles, while the ferry range of the F111 without in-flight refuelling was 4,500 miles, and the operational radius over 1,000 miles. If British defence policy was to become more Eurocentric, the F111 would have more relevance to the Central Front than the CVA-01.

As an offensive system the F111 possessed three distinct advantages over the Royal Navy's Buccaneer:

(i)   the maximum payload of the F111 was 10 tons greater than the Buccaneer, and over long distances the proportion differential increased;
(ii) the better avionics of the F111 allowed it to indulge in terrain-hugging low-level flying, usually at 100–400ft, avoiding ground-based radar;
(iii) the 'swing wings' and low-pressure tyres would have enabled the F111 to operate from short, perhaps rough runways.

It was argued that island runways were vulnerable, and could be put out of action for one to three hours by heavy conventional bombs – but was that really so long?

Despite the fact that the carrier force would be less of a strain on the dollar reserves, overall costs worked in favour of the F111. Costing £2·5m. per unit and £250,000 per year to maintain, the overall cost of operating seventy-five F111s (fifty permanently on the front line) over ten years was reckoned to be approximately £375m. The cost of a two-carrier task force would approach £1,000m. over ten years. Only a minimal amount of the difference would have been required to develop the island bases, and a base in northern Australia. Financial considerations won the day, and the Minister of Defence and Chief of the Defence Staff opted for the F111s. February 1966 saw the formal cancellation of the CVA-01, and an order placed for seventy-five F111s. January 1968 witnessed the cancellation of the F111 order.

The 1970s saw the British military effort increasingly directed towards requirements exclusive to NATO. However, even with an established 'Eurocentric' defence policy operational problems derived from economic constraints persisted, as illustrated by the British decision not to intervene in the Cyprus crisis of 1974 despite two well-furnished bases and a large contingent of troops on the island. In the 1975 Defence Review the Ministry of Defence gave notice, *inter alia*, of its intention to withdraw a permanent RN presence from the Mediterranean while the British reinforcement capability for NATO's northern flank was to be depleted. By 1975 it appeared as if Britain would be a military power of consequence only in continental north-west Europe, in the Channel and in the eastern Atlantic.

Notes: Chapter 3

1 In the 1960s Britain exported one-fifth of its GNP, and until 1967 the Commonwealth was Britain's largest trading partner.
2 Bruce Reed and Geoffrey Williams, *Denis Healey and the Policies of Power* (London: Sidgwick & Jackson, 1971), p. 6.
3 See *Statement on Defence Estimates 1966. Part I. The Defence Review*, Cmnd 2901 (London: HMSO, 1966), pp. 6–7, para. 16, quoted in Laurence Martin, *British Defence Policy: The Long Recessional*, Adelphi Paper No. 61 (London: ISS, 1969), p. 5.
4 See J. D. B. Miller, *Survey of Commonwealth Affairs: Problems of Expansion and Attrition 1953-1969* (London: Oxford University Press, 1974), pp. 360–3.
5 Sir Alec Douglas-Home in the House of Commons, 6 February 1964, quoted in Waldemar A. Nielson, *The Great Powers and Africa* (London: Pall Mall, 1969), p. 61.
6 Quoted in Geoffrey Goodwin, 'British foreign policy since 1945: the long Odyssey to Europe', in Michael Leifer (ed.), *Constraints and Adjustments in British Foreign Policy* (London: Allen & Unwin, 1972), pp. 47–8.
7 See A. J. Pierre, *Nuclear Politics* (London: Oxford University Press, 1972), pp. 285–6.
8 Harold Macmillan, 30 January 1963, House of Commons, *Hansard*, vol. 670, cols 959–60, quoted in Laslo V. Boyd, *Britain's Search for a Role* (Lexington, Mass.: Saxon House/Lexington Books, 1975), pp. 87–8.
9 See *Progress of Five Year Defence Plan 1959*, Cmnd 662 (London: HMSO, 1959), especially the proposed improvements to air mobility and support, pp. 2–3, paras 10–13.

58 The Influence of British Arms

10 See John Baylis, 'British defence policy', in John Baylis *et al.*, *Contemporary Strategy* (London: Croom Helm, 1975), pp. 277–8.

11 *Statement on Defence Estimates 1965*, Cmnd 2592 (London: HMSO, 1965), paras 8 and 9.

12 Reed and Williams, op. cit., pp. 7–8.

13 See ibid., p. 217.

14 Quoted in Coral Bell, 'The Special Relationship', in Leifer (ed.), op. cit., p. 109.

15 Peter Calvocoressi, *The British Experience 1945–1975* (London: The Bodley Head, 1978), p. 215.

16 See Patrick Gordon Walker, *The Cabinet* (London: Jonathan Cape, 1970), pp. 128–9.

17 David Greenwood, 'Constraints and choices in the transformation of Britain's defence effort since 1945', *British Journal of International Studies*, vol. 2, no. 1 (1976), p. 25.

18 See Stephen Kirby, 'Britain's defence policy and NATO', in Leifer (ed.), op. cit., p. 76.

19 John Baylis, 'Defence decision-making in Britain and the determinants of defence policy', *Journal of the Royal United Services Institute for Defence Studies* (hereafter RUSIJ), vol. CXX, no. 1 (1975), p. 45.

20 ibid.

21 *Supplementary Statement on Defence Policy 1967*, Cmnd 3357 (London: HMSO, 1967), para. 1.

22 Elisabeth Barker, *Britain in a Divided Europe 1945–1970* (London: Weidenfeld & Nicolson, 1971), p. 213.

23 See Douglas Hurd, *An End to Promises* (London: Collins, 1979), ch. 4.

24 See *Statement on Defence Estimates 1975*, Cmnd 5976 (London: HMSO, 1975).

25 See P. M. Kennedy, 'British defence policy part II: an historian's view', *RUSIJ*, vol. CXXII, no. 4 (1977), pp. 14–17.

26 Calvocoressi, op. cit., p. 213.

27 *Statement on Defence Estimates 1948*, Cmnd 7327 (London: HMSO, 1948), p. 3, para. 10.

28 See *Defence: Outline of Future Policy 1957*, Cmnd 124 (London: HMSO, 1957).

29 See Martin, op. cit., p. 2.

30 See Antony Verrier, 'British defence policy under Labor', *Foreign Affairs*, vol. 42, no. 2 (1964), p. 284.

31 Reed and Williams, op. cit., p. 203.

32 For a detailed analysis of the defence budgeting process in Britain see David Greenwood, *Budgeting for Defence* (London: RUSI, 1972).

33 See Sir Solly Zuckerman, *Scientists and War* (London: Hamish Hamilton, 1966), p. 45, cited in Joseph Frankel, *British Foreign Policy 1945–1973* (London: Oxford University Press, 1975), pp. 290–1.

34 See Hugh Hanning, 'Britain east of Suez – facts and figures', *International Affairs*, vol. 42, no. 2 (1966), p. 253.

35 Quoted in Christopher Mayhew, *Britain's Role Tomorrow* (London: Hutchinson, 1967), p. 19.

36 See *Statement on Defence Estimates 1967*, Cmnd 3203 (London: HMSO, 1967), p. 7, para. 26.

37 See David Owen, *The Politics of Defence* (London: Jonathan Cape, 1972), p. 102.

38 *Statement on Defence Estimates 1968*, Cmnd 3540 (London: HMSO, 1968), p. 2, para. 3(a).

39 See Michael Howard, 'British defence policy and the future of the armed forces', *RUSIJ*, vol. CXIII, no. 4 (1968), p. 288.

40 See Michael Howard, 'Britain's defenses: commitments and capabilities', *Foreign Affairs*, vol. 39, no. 1 (1960), p. 83.

41 Air Marshal Sir M. Heath, 'The balance of Britain's air power', *RUSIJ*, vol. CXI, no. 2 (1966), p. 125.

42 Phillip Darby, *British Defence Policy, East of Suez 1947–1968* (London: Oxford University Press, 1973), p. 184.

43 See Neville Brown, 'The Carrier or the F111?' *New Scientist*, 27 January 1966, pp. 205–6.

4 *Interventions*

In the decade following Suez, and contrary to the expectations epitomised by the 1957 Defence White Paper, Britain found itself exercising military force outside the NATO area in a number of limited military conflicts or political crises. The conflicts and crises to be examined were invariably hangovers from Empire, and British national interests, whether tangible such as oil, or intangible such as prestige and status, were perceived to be in need of protection. In this period most policy-makers viewed Britain as in the ranks of the great powers, if not quite the equal of the United States and the Soviet Union, and with the concomitant responsibility to contribute towards stability in the international system. The apparent success of interventions undertaken between 1957 and 1966 was often used by spokesmen of both major parties to vindicate Britain's claim to a 'unique' international role, and justify the allocation of scarce resources to the projection of stability-inducing military power beyond the North Atlantic.

The lessons of the Suez experience were appreciated, and great care was taken not to repeat such a disaster, even on a lesser scale, but none the less these 'successful' interventions contain important notes of caution for medium-rank powers contemplating repeat performances, alone or in coalition.

July 1957: Oman

The first three cases of intervention following Suez are of particular interest as they took place in the Middle East – a region where Britain had lost much prestige, and was not generally popular. The first intervention, less than a year after Suez, was in the Persian Gulf, an area of traditional British influence.

On 17 July 1957 the Sultan of Muscat requested British military aid to assist in quelling a revolt involving the Imam of Oman. Invited by a recognised, sovereign ruler in a region long acknowledged to be of considerable strategic and economic importance to Britain, the Macmillan government had little hesitation in dispatching aid. There was no political disagreement in Britain, the objective of maintaining the sultan in power was clear, and the operation was expected to be over and completed relatively quickly. Indeed, by 12 August a combination of forces comprising British infantry (the Cameronians), RAF Venom and Shackleton aircraft, British-officered Trucial Oman Scouts, RN frigates and the sultan's own forces had removed the immediate threat, but the rebels were not totally defeated. They were driven into the mountains of the Hajor range, in particular the rugged Jebel Akhdar, where it took a long campaign, including many unsuccessful attacks, to eventually expel the rebel forces by January 1959. Two hundred and fifty British troops, including the Special Air Service (the final operation of the campaign is reputed to have saved the SAS from disbandment) and over eight hundred of the sultan's forces were required to scale the Jebel and defeat the rebels.

The campaign took eighteen months, and experienced several operational and logistical problems. British troops suffered considerably from the heat and army vehicles could not operate to full capacity. The crisis broke out on 17 July, but it took nineteen days for British forces to arrive in enough strength to begin operations.[1] One company of Cameronians was based in Bahrain but, owing to the shortage of air-conditioned accommodation, the other two were based in Kenya and had to be air-transported to the Gulf without benefit of proper acclimatisation. RAF bombing of rebel villages and strongholds and the effective blockade of seaborne arms supplies to the rebels by the Royal Navy put a decisive end to the threat.[2] Nevertheless, if the initial challenge against the sultan had been marginally stronger and better organised, then the small number of British forces could have found themselves bogged down for even longer, suffering greater casualties from the climate and the enemy than occurred; and hence the intervention would not have been quite so 'successful'.

July 1958: Jordan

In July 1958 a *coup d'état* overthrew the pro-Western administration of King Faisal II of Iraq and, among others, the king and his prime minister were assassinated by radical, pro-Moscow forces. The young King Hussein in Jordan feared that his rule would crumble in the face of the Iraqi example and Egyptian anti-Hashemite propaganda but, in the post-Suez atmosphere of 1957, defence treaty ties with Britain had been abrogated. At the same time as Hussein searched for support so did the Lebanon, also fearing the example set in Iraq. The result was that Beirut invited United States military intervention, and Amman invited British military intervention, to deter any anti-monarchist, Iraqi-inspired revolt. On 15 July marines from the United States Sixth Fleet waded ashore in the Lebanon, and on the 17th British forces began to arrive in Jordan.[3]

Altogether 1,500 troops were flown into Jordan, Hunter fighters arrived to support the ground forces and a brigade was moved to Cyprus in reserve. The British forces remained until early November, and then departed when the Hussein government appeared stable and secure. The lessons of the Suez expedition had not been contravened but, in addition, the results of the intervention appeared all the more attractive because not only did the United

States not oppose it as an example of West European imperialism, but on this occasion it worked in unison with Britain in keeping the peace in an area of great strategic and economic importance for the West.

However, though welcomed by the Jordanian authorities, and operating in a friendly environment, risks were run and logistic hurdles encountered. The initial small force of paratroopers found themselves alone in Jordan for twelve hours, unsure and concerned about the loyalty of the Jordanian army. Reinforcements were delayed by over-flight objections by the Israeli government. Forces from Kenya were still arriving by 7 August, and it was 10 August before their vehicles arrived: 'The Jordan operation in 1958, when a brigade was despatched to offer protection against Egyptian threats, exposed continued deficiencies in the strategic reserve and in the provision of air transport to make it effective.' [4]

June/July 1961: Kuwait

The notion of Britain's unique role in contributing to international stability and the protection of Western interests, especially in regions in which Britain traditionally wielded influence, notably the Persian Gulf, is conveyed by the following extracts from an article in a widely read international affairs journal:

> Britain in the Persian Gulf today occupies the dual position of residual legatee of the past and common trustee of the present. She has obligations to fulfil arising out of her historical connection with the Gulf, and vital interests to defend in the shape of large-scale oil investment, not only of her own but those of Europe and the United States as well. Beyond that her presence in the Gulf is part of the defensive strategy of the West and a contribution to the maintenance of peace and order in this part of the world. [5]

> She [Britain] is no less bound by the responsibilities laid upon her by the past, in particular the defence of the minor principalities against their enemies and, what is sometimes obscured, a duty to ensure their emergence into the modern world as credible states and not as medieval anachronisms. These obligations cannot be shrugged off because they may be uncomfortable or because they may expose Britain to criticism. Still less can Britain evade her responsibility to herself, to her allies, and to the world at large to continue to contribute to the upholding of peace, order and the rule of law in an area to which she, and she alone, brought all three. [6]

These notions of 'role', 'duty', and 'history' east of Suez were reinforced by the publicly acclaimed success of the role of British arms in the Kuwait crisis of July 1961.

Between 1899 and 1961 an Anglo-Kuwait Treaty had provided British protection for the Gulf state. In the 1960s, as this was seen not to be in keeping with the status of a wealthy, sovereign Arab state, the 1899 Treaty was replaced with an exchange of letters,[7] fulfilling, in reality, very much the same function as the treaty, but much more diplomatically acceptable. To Britain, especially since the Iraqi *coup* of 1958, Kuwait was one of the most important states in the Middle East. Kuwait contained some 21 per cent of the world's proven oil reserves, and production costs were much lower than elsewhere in the Middle East or South America. In 1960, in terms of volume, Kuwait provided Britain with 38·27 per cent of total oil imports. Furthermore, 50 per cent of the Kuwait Oil Company was owned by BP, its transactions were conducted in sterling and the reserves were deposited in London.[8]

Upon the cessation of the Anglo-Kuwait Treaty, Iraq began to threaten the integrity of Kuwait, and laid claim to Kuwait as 'a long lost but integral part of Iraq'.[9] On 30 June Sheikh Abdullah of Kuwait formally requested British assistance. The British feared not only invasion from Iraq, but internal subversion and a *coup d'état* perhaps on the Egyptian and Iraqi model. With the full Cabinet in support Macmillan decided to intervene,[10] spurred by reports from the British embassy in Baghdad of ominous military movements and by increasingly hostile Iraqi propaganda.

Within the first two weeks of July 6,000 British troops, with stores and equipment, arrived in Kuwait, mostly by air. Two squadrons of Hunters and some Canberra bombers arrived, as well as *Bulwark*, the commando carrier. To Britain's advantage, much of Arab opinion was cool towards Iraq and, if not enthusiastically supportive of Britain's intervention, at least did not oppose it. Saudi Arabia had territorial disputes with Iraq. Nasser resented Iraqi pretensions to the radical leadership of the Arab world, while many Arab states were suspicious of Baghdad's close relations with Moscow. By 16 October the Arab League provided a force of 3,000 to replace the British forces deployed in Kuwait.[11] British military strength had successfully deterred the threat to Kuwait from Iraq, and British bases in the Gulf and on the periphery of the Indian Ocean facilitated the intervention. The Kuwait intervention appeared to vindicate Britain's east of Suez policy: 'It afforded an admirable example of the effective use of a small British force if its deployment was rapid and timely.'[12]

There can be no doubt that the intervention was successful: Kassem of Iraq was deterred, and considerable care was taken to avoid any Suez-type débâcle. Macmillan secured full Cabinet support, the United States was in favour and Iraq was isolated in the Arab world. But an examination of the operation illustrates again the difficulties of long-range intervention, even when a great many factors are in the favour of the intervening power. As most of the Arab world did not support Iraq in this particular quarrel British vessels could use the Suez Canal and there were few over-flight problems but, nevertheless, it was thirteen days after Sheikh Abdullah's request for military assistance when all the British forces – ground, naval and air – were deployed. HMS *Bulwark*, the commando carrier, was, conveniently and coincidentally, in Karachi on 29 June, while HMS *Striker*, of the Amphibious Warfare Squadron, with half a squadron of the 3rd Dragoon Guards and their Centurion tanks on board, was patrolling in the Gulf, out of Aden.

The Kuwait operation of 1961 is often used as a 'good example' of the capabilities of strategic transport. But although 6,000 troops were moved in the first six days of the crisis, this was achieved only by chartering seventeen civil aircraft and employing three transports of the Royal Rhodesian Air Force. Only 70 tons of equipment and supplies were moved by air, the remainder by sea.[13] The political success of the operation disguised the inadequacies of the strategic air-lift.

Kuwait was very vulnerable strategically, and in terms of numbers and equipment the British forces would have been very hard pressed if hostilities had broken out, particularly in the early days of the crisis. Acclimatisation, a factor often overlooked in military operations, was also a grave problem. In the intense heat of the Gulf 137 British personnel suffered from heat exhaustion during the period of the intervention.[14]

The British presence lasted just over three months – not particularly long – but even by then the local welcome had turned into a kind of resentment over Kuwaiti dependence upon British protection. The Kuwait intervention, though politically successful, has considerable significance as an example of the difficulties and risks of the long-range projection of military power, even in relatively favourable circumstances.

December 1963: Cyprus

The hazards of intervention were evident when British forces found themselves fulfilling a peace-keeping role in the troublesome former colony of Cyprus in the winter of 1963/4. Fighting had broken out between the Greek (80 per cent of the population) and Turkish (20 per cent of the population and spread throughout the island in small villages) communities, and British forces were not only invited by President Makarios to intervene but, by the Treaty of Guarantee,[15] by which Britain, Greece and Turkey could take joint or individual action to maintain the status quo, had every right (and an obligation) to do so. British troops were on the island in the sovereign bases agreed at the time of independence in 1960, and used the island for training purposes, but little could be done when fighting broke out on 21 December 1963. Greek and Turkish troops on the island assisted the respective communities, and refused to join with the British in restoring order.

In 1964 the Cyprus bases were of considerable strategic significance, as staging posts to the Gulf and the Far East, as bases for the V-bomber strategic deterrent, as a training area for forces, as an important communications centre and as a valuable contribution to NATO's south-eastern flank.[16] But these functions could not be implemented properly, if at all, if there was wide-spread internal unrest on the island.

British troops already on the island could do little more than assess the problem and protect service families, though occasionally a local ceasefire could be arranged. Between 29 December 1963 and 5 January 1964 three units of infantry were flown in from Britain, and a squadron of armoured cars from Libya, but even with reinforcements British forces were inadequate for proper policing and peace-keeping. With British forces committed around the globe London was desperate to spread the burden, and appealed in January to the United Nations. Political problems at the United Nations over the financing of the peace-keeping forces, and the British determination to prevent Soviet and East European forces from gaining access to the island under United Nations auspices, complicated and delayed the United Nations assumption of the task. Eventually, by 2 March, the United Nations reached agreement on the composition and other details of an international peace-keeping force, but the immediate result of this was an increase in the fighting by the Greek Cypriots, with the British forces in the middle of it, in an effort to maximise their positions before the United Nations peace-keeping force arrived. On 27 March the British forces, some of which joined the United Nations force, transferred peace-keeping duties to the United Nations force, eventually composed of Swedish, Irish, Finnish, Austrian and Canadian troops under the command of an Indian, General Gyani.

However, for three months British forces had found themselves over-stretched and overworked, increasingly unpopular as Greeks and Turks turned their frustrations against them.[17] The British troops available were inadequate for the task, except to minimise the casualties and do the best they could on the spot: 'it was proved at Limassol on February 13th, when the Greeks set savagely upon the Turks, that there could be no stopping determined attacks without the prior deployment of posts, and the force available was absurdly inadequate for the prevention of such attacks'.[18] At this time, with British forces in action in East Africa and Malaysia, overstretch was hardly surprising. British intervention undoubtedly did prevent some blood-shed, and was a calming influence – on the island, and between Greece and Turkey – but the Cyprus intervention highlights the difficulty of keeping the peace between bitter foes. Even the United Nations force (UNFICYP), 7,000 strong, did not have enough men to do the job adequately, and soon became unpopular. It was not a job the British forces enjoyed, nor one for which they were equipped or trained. Using arms only for self-defence while attempting to keep the peace between rival factions was found to be a trying task.

January 1964: East Africa

As British soldiers were striving to maintain some semblance of order in Cyprus, emergencies in three newly independent states in East Africa,

Uganda, Tanganyika and Kenya, all former British colonies, resulted in British military intervention. With the bloody Congo crisis still vivid in peoples' memories the success of these interventions was seen by many in both major parties in Britain as another vindication of Britain's military role outside NATO.

In reality, the emergencies comprised ill-organised social protests taking the form of mutinies over conditions in the new armies of the new states. There was no direct political threat or challenge to the recognised political authority of any of the East African states on the Oman or Kuwait model. However, it is fair to argue that the mutinies, if unchecked, could have led to considerable political disturbance, and perhaps the fall of governments.

On 23 January a large part of the Ugandan army mutinied. Three days previously a mutiny led by sergeants had broken out in Tanganyika. As the Ugandan and Tanganyikan armies had been parts of the same regiment there were fears that the troubles in Tanganyika would spread. Sir David Hunt, British High Commissioner in Kampala, saw Dr Milton Obote, the Ugandan prime minister, early on the 23rd and 'hinted that if trouble should come he had friends whom he could rely on'.[19] In the late afternoon soldiers at Jinja barracks refused to obey orders. At 5.45 Obote held a conference, and at 6.00 he called the British High Commission to make an official request 'for the intervention of British troops to secure Entebbe airfield, to safeguard vital installations in Entebbe and Kampala and to assist the Ugandan Government to preserve peace'.[20] After asking for the request in writing,[21] Hunt contacted London, which instructed a battalion of the North Staffordshire regiment to fly into Entebbe from Kenya that evening. The following morning, without bloodshed, British forces disarmed the mutineers.

Although the potential for a political explosion was present because of the conflict between Obote and the Kabaka of Buganda,[22] an indigenous monarch, the basis of the Ugandan mutiny was pay and conditions in the army. The Ugandan army, at independence, was one thousand strong, but it only had nine Ugandan officers, all previously senior serving soldiers. In 1961 there was only one Ugandan cadet at Sandhurst, though by 1963 twelve were in training or on their way to Britain. In 1964 the Ugandan army was still officered, on the whole, by British officers, and there was discontent over pay differentials between the ranks. While visiting the mutineers the Minister for Internal Affairs was forced to sign a document authorising a massive pay increase – hardly the action of revolutionaries. The Obote government had already announced an interim pay increase for the higher ranks but, imprudently, only a vague review for the rest. The well-being of the armed forces was a low-priority issue: 'This was a reflection of a typical lack of appreciation by African politicians of their armed forces which long after independence they tend to see as relics of imperialism and not really their own: in the Uganda case it might have proved disastrous to the new state without, ironically, the assistance of British troops.'[23]

Following the Ugandan mutiny some soldiers were dismissed, but a pay increase was awarded and the decision to Africanise senior posts was taken. At that time both the battalion and army commanders were British. An African commanding officer was appointed – a man who had acted commendably throughout the mutiny – Lt. Col. Idi Amin.

News from Tanganyika and Uganda sparked off a mutiny in Kenya, but with British troops to hand, and little reluctance by Kenyatta to call upon their assistance, it posed a small threat to the Nairobi government's survival. In Kenya the Africanisation of the senior ranks was relatively advanced, and only a small proportion of the army was involved in the mutiny. Dissident elements of the 11th Battalion Kenyan Rifles were arrested. About 100 were court-martialled and severely punished, and another 170 were dismissed from the army.[24] A new unit was formed, including members of the youth wing of the Kenyan African National Union.

It was in Tanganyika, the location of the first of the mutinies, that the gravest political threat to the government emerged. A violent and bloody revolution was under way in Zanzibar, within sight of Dar es Salaam, when the mutiny broke out at Colito barracks on 20 January. There was genuine surprise at the mutiny because if any disturbance was expected it was internecine conflict within the Tanganyikan African National Union, the sole and official political party, which spread itself very wide, and had more field workers than the army had soldiers.[25]

Pay and conditions were at the root of the troubles in the Tanganyikan army, including the slow rate of Africanisation of the senior ranks. By the end of 1963 there were still twenty-nine British officers in the Tanganyikan army, including all those above the rank of major. There was a British plan for the 'localisation' of the officer corps before 1965 but the Nyerere government exhibited little urgency over the matter.

Nyerere was out of the capital when the mutineers took over control of the key areas of Dar es Salaam, and assumed control up-country at Tabara and Nachingwea. Nyerere and his ministers, except Oscar Kambona, Minister of External Affairs and Defence, went into hiding. Kambona received the mutineers' demands which were exclusively about pay, conditions and the replacement of British by African officers, and were not at all political: 'Any question of external advice and support is unproven. If any member of the Government was directly implicated then it is surprising that, when a genuine power vacuum had been created, a take-over was not effected: the same would not be true if foreign subversion had been involved.'[26]

Nyerere emerged from hiding on 21 January, attempting to play down the mutiny, and on the 22nd toured Dar es Salaam. However, reports of police discontent, news of what was happening in Kenya and Uganda, and fears that anti-Nyerere elements would try to politicise the disruption finally persuaded Nyerere to invite British military intervention. Initially Nyerere was loath to request the assistance of the former colonial power, but the precedents of Kenya and Uganda eased his humiliation.

On 25 January Royal Marine commandos from the carrier HMS *Centaur* landed, and competently and efficiently, with the minimum of bloodshed, rounded up the mutineers, some trade union leaders who attempted to use the crisis to force Nyerere to lift restrictions on union activity and some discontented policemen. When the British forces withdrew a Nigerian battalion temporarily took over. The mutinous soldiers were simply dismissed, leaving a very weak Tanganyikan army for a number of years.

1963–6: Malaysia

In August 1962 the Malayan and British governments announced their intention to establish the Federation of Malaysia the following year. The federation was to include Singapore, Sarawak and North Borneo. In the elections of June 1963 the people of Brunei opted to remain out of any federation, full control of their own oil revenues being a major factor in their decision. Although the United Nations concluded that the proposed federation was a major issue in the elections in North Borneo and Sarawak and hence had the support of the majority of the populations, Indonesia and the Philippines, both of which had territorial claims against the new federation, objected strongly. On 15 September 1963, the day before the Federation of Malaysia was established, both Indonesia and the Philippines broke off diplomatic relations, but the military threat to the new state emanated only from Indonesia. President Sukarno, who had grand visions of a greater Indonesia, had been pursuing a war of words prior to the establishment of the federation, accusing the Malayan government of neo-colonialism and of connivance with the former imperial power. On 21 September Indonesia broke off economic relations with Malaysia in an attempt to damage the port of Singapore. In reality this was rather an unwise strategy as the countries which constituted the federation accounted for about half Indonesia's export trade.

Sukarno's antagonism, which led to military 'Confrontation', was based upon a mix of foreign and domestic policy objectives, with the domestic predominant. In foreign affairs Sukarno wished to align Indonesia with Peking, and did not want Western military forces based near his borders hindering Indonesian expansion and the projection of influence. Inside Indonesia Sukarno was encountering an array of economic and political problems and the Confrontation was a device to distract attention: 'His balancing of political forces at home, whether between personalities in the government and the armed forces, or between one political party and another, or between the armed forces and the Communists, demanded a restless style of rule, especially since the Indonesian economy was in decline.' [27]

The British military presence in the new Federation of Malaysia and the use of British military forces to counter the Indonesian incursions were legitimised by the Anglo-Malayan Defence and Mutual Assistance Agreement of 1957 (whereby Australia and New Zealand were also committed to provide troops in the event of hostilities) which was extended to include the states of the federation.[28] The defence of a 1,000-mile frontier and a 3,000-mile coastline was a daunting task, but there was an immediate agreement between the British, Australian and New Zealand governments that Indonesian aggression must be contained. By late 1963 and early 1964 there were many incursions into Malaysia from Indonesia, supposedly by 'volunteers', but actually by Indonesian army regulars in 'volunteer' uniform. In reality, the euphemism 'Confrontation', which Sukarno had coined in January 1963, many months before the federation actually came into existence, disguised acts of war.

However, in certain ways, the opportunities provided by the Confrontation were attractive to British policy-makers. As with Kuwait and East Africa, it was used to vindicate and justify a British military role and presence east of Suez while, simultaneously, it created a natural division of labour with the United States in 'keeping the peace' in South-East Asia, and an acceptable excuse for Britain not to get involved in the Vietnam imbroglio.[29] Britain was much more sceptical of images of grand Moscow—Peking plots in South-East Asia than the United States, or even Australia, which liked to see itself as a bridge between the United States and Britain in South-East Asian affairs. Britain's main concern was the port and financial centre of Singapore, and British commercial interests in Malaysia as a whole, totalling over £800 million.

Confrontation cost few lives (300 Commonwealth casualties, 114 of which were fatal) for the number of troops deployed, but in other ways it was very expensive. The large Indonesian force, equipped with Mig21s, Badger bombers and missile-firing destroyers (such advanced equipment was usually poorly maintained), was seen to pose a considerable threat to Malaysia. Hence a large British military presence was essential, mainly by the army, but also by the Royal Navy, required to patrol the Straits of Malacca and to defend the long, vulnerable Malaysian coastline. At the height of the Confrontation Britain had 59,000 military personnel[30] in Malaysia, its largest military force in the Far East since the Korean War, and at one point there were more than six infantry battalions based in Borneo. The Far East fleet built up to a strength of some eighty vessels, including aircraft carriers and, for a spell, the Royal Air Force presence was reinforced by the visit of some V-bombers to Singapore – an event which raised the prospect of the ultimate deterrent against any Indonesian escalation of the conflict.

The Confrontation of 1963–6 is estimated to have cost £256 million[31] but, nevertheless, there was no domestic opposition to the commitment:

When the role of defender of Malaysia was assumed by the Labour administration of Harold Wilson it served as a valuable symbol for a political party which felt a need to demonstrate its national credentials. What could be better than to stand by a justifiably aggrieved Commonwealth country which, at the time, could be represented as a model in race relations and parliamentary democratic practice.[32]

Fully aware that the charge of neo-colonialism could be easily levelled, even though it was inaccurate, the British government wanted a short, low-profile military presence.[33] Consequently, great care was taken to limit fire-power, and novel operational techniques were used. Unusually, the defending European army, though Gurkha troops were used extensively, found itself adopting guerrilla tactics to combat the enemy:

> Air superiority was used only for reconnaissance, mobility and supply, to discourage escalation, the basic fighting being the work of well-trained, well-handled infantry, who set out to out-guerrilla the guerrilla. Helicopters were used to land troops, not amid the enemy, but near the scene to set up ambushes or outflanking moves in secrecy.[34]

Great care was taken to win the 'hearts and minds' of the local population, not only to gain their political support, but to tap their knowledge for intelligence purposes – good intelligence being the basis of any successful counter-guerrilla campaign.

By 1966 the Confrontation was over, but whether this was more a result of the defensive and deterrent power of British military force or of the internal domestic difficulties[35] (produced, in part, by the Confrontation policy) which overwhelmed Sukarno is a matter of considerable debate. On the issue of deterrence one point worthy of note is that the pre-Confrontation presence of British forces, as part of the Commonwealth Strategic Reserve, did not deter Sukarno's initial hostility, and a much larger, high profile presence, even though the campaign was low key, was required to bring the conflict to an end. For whatever reasons, British military intervention was successful, but it contributed considerably to the global overstretch of British forces, and if the Confrontation had escalated into a Vietnam-type conflict then Britain would not have had the resources to sustain a prolonged, active presence.

On 1 June 1966 the Bangkok Accord was signed normalising relations between Indonesia and Malaysia, and on 11 August a peace pact was agreed between the two states in Jakarta.[36] Sukarno was still president but his political position was weakening daily. There had been an attempted *coup d'état* in September 1965 which, although it had failed, brought about a change in the Indonesian power structure. General Suharto became the real authority in Indonesia following an army-led counter *coup* a month later. It was Suharto's policy to run down the Confrontation as soon as political conditions in Indonesia allowed it. Suharto removed Sukarno from the presidency in early 1967, conducted a bloody anti-communist purge and adopted a pro-Western foreign policy posture.

It is fair to argue that British military opposition to the Confrontation has contributed towards the stability of that part of South-East Asia. Together with Kuwait and the East African emergencies in particular, the Confrontation was widely cited as a vindication of Britain's worldwide defence commitments, and its unique role – Britain was the only state in the world which was not suspected of acquisitive designs when its armed forces answered requests to maintain stability and security in the developing world. However, although the British intervention in the Confrontation was hailed as a great success there was also considerable relief when it came to an end, and a determination not to get involved in such a large-scale and potentially enormous commitment again. The years of the Confrontation, intervention in the Gulf and East Africa, and not forgetting demanding colonial peace-keeping duties in territories such as British Guiana and Aden (e.g. between 1963 and 1968, 68 British soldiers were killed and 669 wounded in Aden),[37] produced considerable manpower and other resource overstretch. During this period the British Army of the Rhine had to be depleted of manpower to meet demands outside NATO. If the Confrontation had escalated then the strain on British military and economic resources could have proved unbearable, resulting in the abandonment of a former colony to disruption and subversion and the humiliating refusal by Britain to respond to pleas for military assistance. By 1967, despite the political will, economic stringency and related operational problems decreed that the Confrontation was to be the last classic British military intervention.

Notes: Chapter 4

1 See Gregory Blaxland, *The Regiments Depart* (London: William Kimber, 1971), p. 355.
2 See C. G. Bartlett, *The Long Retreat* (London: Macmillan, 1972), p. 164.
3 See Blaxland, op. cit., pp. 349−51.
4 William Wallace, 'World status without tears', in V. Bogdanor and R. Skidelsky (eds), *The Age of Affluence 1951−1964* (London: Macmillan, 1970), p. 216.
5 J. B. Kelly, 'The British position in the Persian Gulf', *The World Today*, vol. 20, no. 6 (1964), p. 238.
6 ibid., pp. 248−9.
7 See Harold Macmillan, *Pointing the Way 1959−1961* (London: Macmillan, 1972), p. 383.
8 See Peter Mangold, 'Britain and the defence of Kuwait 1956−71', *RUSIJ*, vol. CXX, no. 3 (1975), pp. 44−5.
9 See Macmillan, op. cit.
10 ibid., p. 385.
11 See Lincoln Bloomfield, *The United Nations and United States Foreign Policy* (London: University of London Press, 1969), p. 81.
12 Macmillan, op. cit., p. 387.
13 See P. Darby, *British Defence Policy East of Suez 1947−1968* (London: Oxford University Press for the Royal Institute for International Affairs, 1973), p. 247.
14 See Blaxland, op. cit., p. 361.
15 See Andrew Boyd, *Fifteen Men on a Powder Keg* (London: Methuen, 1973), p. 277.
16 See Antony Verrier, 'Cyprus: Britain's security role', *The World Today*, vol. 20, no. 3 (1964), pp. 131−7.
17 See Nancy Crawshaw, *The Cyprus Revolt* (London: Allen & Unwin, 1978), p. 368.
18 Blaxland, op. cit., p. 326.
19 Sir David Hunt, *On the Spot* (London: Peter Davies, 1975), p. 147.
20 ibid., p. 148.
21 Mentioned in a letter to *The Times* by Sir David Hunt, 25 August 1978.

22 See William F. Gutteridge, *The Military in African Politics* (London: Methuen, 1969), p. 13.
23 ibid., p. 37.
24 ibid., p. 34.
25 See Frene Ginwala, 'The Tanganyikan mutiny', *The World Today*, vol. 20, no. 3 (1964), pp. 93–7.
26 Gutteridge, op. cit., p. 29.
27 J. D. B. Miller, *Survey of Commonwealth Affairs, Problems of Expansion and Attrition* (London: Oxford University Press, 1974), p. 85.
28 See Richard Allen, *Malaysia: Prospect and Retrospect* (London: Oxford University Press, 1968), p. 153.
29 See Miller, op. cit., p. 22.
30 See David Owen, *The Politics of Defence* (London: Jonathan Cape, 1972), p. 98.
31 See Joseph Frankel, *British Foreign Policy 1948–1973* (London: Oxford University Press, 1975), p. 302.
32 Michael Leifer, 'Retreat and reappraisal in South East Asia', in Michael Leifer (ed.), *Constraints and Adjustments in British Foreign Policy* (London: Allen & Unwin, 1972), p. 88.
33 For details of the operations see Blaxland, op. cit., pp. 395–410.
34 Bartlett, op. cit., p. 187.
35 See David Vital, *The Making of British Foreign Policy* (London: Allen & Unwin, 1968), pp. 25–6.
36 See Michael Leifer, 'Indonesia and Malaysia: the changing face of Confrontation', *The World Today*, vol. 22, no. 9 (1966), pp. 395–405.
37 See Blaxland, op. cit., p. 464.

5 Non-Intervention: 1966—74

In the decade following Suez there were a number of British military interventions, over and above colonial peace-keeping and withdrawal exercises, which were often cited as a vindication of Britain's extra-North Atlantic role and fine examples of the contribution Britain could make to international stability and security. However, from the mid-1960s to the mid-1970s there was a period when a number of extra-European crises arose in response to which British military intervention might have been expected, or even requested, but did not take place. There are two outstanding cases of British military non-intervention: (i) the Rhodesian rebellion of 1965, and (ii) the Cyprus crisis of 1974. Non-intervention, particularly military non-intervention, is important and worthy of attention because, if it is expected by international treaty but does not occur, then a policy statement is being made perhaps of greater significance than if a state resorted to the use of arms as expected, invited, or legally obliged. Military non-intervention does not preclude, and may even spawn, other forms of intervention. For example, in the Nigerian Civil War of 1967—70 some viewed the continued recognition of the federal government in Lagos as the government of the whole of Nigeria, including Biafra, as intervention of a sort, while supporters of the federal government would undoubtedly have viewed a policy of neutrality and equal dealings with the Lagos and Biafran governments as intervention.

What powers with interests at stake do not do is often as important as what they actually do:

> When he was asked the meaning of 'non-intervention', Talleyrand ineffably replied that it was a word, metaphysical and political, which means the same as intervention.[1]

Though the other forms of intervention may have occurred, such as diplomatic intervention, military non-intervention in the two notable cases mentioned above signified definite policy statements by the British government of the day. They conveyed the message that not only was the intervention environment no longer conducive to the long-range projection of military force, but the requisites for a successful intervention, established at Suez, were not present in such a way as to justify the unavoidable risks.

In the years since 1965 Britain has appeared to be adjusting itself to the fact that, as a medium-rank European power, it is no longer in the business of achieving foreign policy objectives outside the North Atlantic area through the projection of military power, but must rely on diplomatic, economic and military aid instruments.

The Rhodesian Rebellion

In 1965 Southern Rhodesia was not a sovereign independent state in international law, or in the eyes of the international community and, strictly speaking, is outside the terms of reference of this study. However, Southern Rhodesia was a unique colony with nearly all the attributes of a sovereign state. As a self-governing colony since 1923, with a long tradition of responsible government and substantial armed forces apparently loyal to Salisbury, the question facing the British government in November 1965, when the Smith regime made a unilateral declaration of independence, was whether to intervene with military force or not. For all practical purposes, Southern Rhodesia had long acted, and was acting, as if it was a completely sovereign state.

Since 1923, when the British South Africa Company, which had administered Southern Rhodesia from the early 1890s, passed responsibility to the British government, Southern Rhodesia had been a self-governing colony, unlike Northern Rhodesia (Zambia) and Nyasaland (Malawi), which were Crown colonies under direct supervision from London. Thus London had no established means of exercising direct control over the Rhodesian government of the day. The image of Southern Rhodesia as a *de facto* sovereign state was enforced by the traditional presence of Rhodesian prime ministers at Imperial and Commonwealth conferences, and the fact that formal relations between London and Salisbury were not conducted through the Colonial Office, but through the Dominions and Commonwealth Relations Office.[2] Rhodesia had its own courts, own police, own civil service, own revenues and own defence forces, and Rhodesians had their own passports. The only times Imperial British troops had ever been in Southern Rhodesia was in 1896 when a Matabele uprising required their presence, and during the Second World War when the RAF used Southern Rhodesia for training purposes. The sense of loyalty to Salisbury rather than to London can be gauged from the fact that out of some twelve thousand civil servants in Rhodesia, only thirty-six resigned after UDI.[3]

Under the 1961 constitution, negotiated between London and Salisbury, London gave up the reserve powers by which it could veto discriminatory legislation and the British government accepted that no Westminster legislation could apply to Southern Rhodesia without the consent of the Salisbury government. The 1961 constitution made Southern Rhodesia a *de facto* sovereign state:

> Sir Edgar Whitehead, who negotiated the 1961 Constitution with the British Government, claimed that Rhodesia was virtually independent.

Legal niceties apart, he was right: the only circumstances in which Britain might conceivably interfere in Rhodesian affairs was if the Rhodesian Government blatantly infringed the Constitution, for example, by a unilateral declaration of independence.[4]

That being the case, why did the Rhodesian Front Party of Ian Smith induce a crisis by declaring UDI in 1965? There are two major related reasons. First, with the failure of the Central African Federation in 1963 and full independence for Southern Rhodesia's two federation partners, Northern Rhodesia and Nyasaland, in 1964, the strong white nationalist movement in Southern Rhodesia gathered force. Its determination was strengthened by the fact that both Northern Rhodesia and Nyasaland had been Crown colonies, not even self-governing. If they gained full sovereignty, then so should Southern Rhodesia. The second and related reason was the problem of the 1961 constitution. It provided *de facto* sovereignty for Southern Rhodesia but also introduced some native African representation into the Salisbury legislature. Fifteen African representatives joined the legislature while the remaining fifty MPs were elected by a franchise based upon income and educational qualifications.[5] The Rhodesian Front was not enthusiastic about the 1961 constitution, but as for the foreseeable future political power would remain in white hands it was accepted by the Rhodesian Front as the basis for independence. Anyway, constitutional change required only a two-thirds majority in parliament, which the Rhodesian Front had after the May 1965 election. However, the British government was prepared to grant full independence only if liberal changes were made to the 1961 constitution which would facilitate African political progress and protect the advance towards majority rule. Such conditions were unacceptable to the Rhodesian Front, and acted as a spur to white Rhodesian nationalism which clamoured for the status of independence.

Relations between London and Salisbury deteriorated considerably between 1963 and 1965, especially after the Wilson government came to power in October 1964. In 1965 the Labour government enunciated five principles which had to be agreed before full independence could be granted to Southern Rhodesia:[6]

(i)   the principle and intention of unimpeded progress to majority rule, already enshrined in the 1961 constitution, would have to be maintained and guaranteed;

(ii) there would also have to be guarantees against retrogressive amendment of the constitution;

(iii) there would have to be immediate improvement in the political status of the African population;

(iv) there would have to be progress towards ending racial discrimination;

(v)   the British government would need to be satisfied that any basis proposed for independence was acceptable to the people of Rhodesia as a whole.

Despite prolonged negotiations in the autumn of 1965, and visits by Smith to London and Wilson to Salisbury, no agreement emerged. On 11 November 1965 the Smith government in Salisbury made a unilateral declaration of independence.

The probability of military intervention was ruled out by the Wilson government even before UDI. On 1 November in the House of Commons Wilson reported that, in Salisbury in October, he had told Nkomo, Sithole and other African leaders that he regarded it as his duty

> to remove from their minds any idea or any hope they might have had that Rhodesia's constitutional problems were going to be solved by an assertion of military power on our part, whether for the purpose of suspending or amending the 1961 Constitution, of majority rule tomorrow or any other time – or for that matter, in dealing with the situation that would follow an illegal assertion of independence.[7]

To publicly admit that military force would not be used, come what may, was undoubtedly a severe tactical error on Wilson's part. To neutralise the most important foreign policy instrument of last resort which any statesman possesses in the face of a developing crisis gravely weakened any efforts by London to deter Salisbury. In the run-up to UDI the prospect of British military intervention must have worried the senior echelons of the Rhodesian Front Party, until Wilson volunteered the intelligence that under no circumstances would his government use force against Southern Rhodesia.

After the event of UDI the decision was to use economic sanctions. On 11 November, the day of UDI, Wilson in the House of Commons again dismissed the use of force, and outlined the initial economic sanctions to which the 'law-breaking' men of Rhodesia were to be subject:[8]

(i) trade was to be restricted, including a ban on tobacco and sugar purchases which constituted 70 per cent of Rhodesia's exports to Britain;
(ii) arms exports were to cease;
(iii) all aid was to be terminated;
(iv) exchange controls were to be applied;
(v) the export of British capital and access to British capital markets were to be disallowed;
(vi) credit guarantees were no longer to be available;
(vii) Rhodesia was to be suspended from the Commonwealth preference area.

Southern Rhodesia was to be brought to its knees as quickly as possible and at a tolerable cost. However, one under-appreciated consequence of the use of economic sanctions was, gradually, to multilateralise the issue. The use of such indirect means necessitated compliance by other nations not directly involved in the Rhodesian constitutional crisis, such as the EEC nations, and some nations not in sympathy with British aims, such as Portugal and the Republic of South Africa. Furthermore, not only the viability but also the justice of sanctions came into question. The level of sacrifice for Zambia, whose economy was closely linked to and dependent upon that of Southern Rhodesia, was far above that borne by Britain and other participating parties in pursuit of effective economic sanctions. Anyway, if economic sanctions had worked as expected, and the social and economic infrastructure of Southern Rhodesia had reached the point of collapse, would British troops not have been required in a policing and peace-keeping role following the surrender?

In the eyes of international public opinion the moral and legal grounds for British military intervention were sound, and neighbouring black African states were willing to offer over-flying rights and whatever operational assistance they could manage. When it became obvious that the British government had decided against the use of the military instrument there was considerable criticism, disappointment and some disillusionment, especially but not exclusively among the black Commonwealth states. Canada had some sympathy for the black African perspective, and supported United Nations action against the Smith regime, incorporating force if required. Australia, aware of its moral vulnerability over its immigration policy and its policy in New Guinea, did not wish to become too involved in the debate and wanted to play down the whole issue. However, in black Africa, anger and disillusionment were widespread. As with Suez, so much was expected of Britain – *the* liberal, decolonising power.

At the December 1965 Commonwealth Parliamentary Association Conference at Wellington delegates from Nigeria, Zambia, India, Jamaica, Uganda, Pakistan, Sierra Leone, Kenya, Tanzania and Trinidad all called for the use of military force against the Smith regime. There was little doubt that international opinion would have supported military intervention. Economic sanctions were derided as ineffective and, as it turned out, such derision was justified. Expressions of majority opinion at the United Nations and the Organisation of African Unity also left little doubt that the developing world attributed British reluctance to use force to racial bias. This produced considerable anti-British bitterness amongst states many of which, as colonies, had experienced a British military presence.

Considering that a number of factors conducive to British military intervention existed, why did the Wilson government decide not to use military force? Two major factors operated to forestall the use of military force, of which one had not been experienced since Suez, and the other was an aggravation of an existing problem. The first was domestic opinion – in the House of Commons, among the general public and, of considerable importance, in the armed forces. The second was military and economic overstretch – too many demands were already being made on British arms and resources elsewhere to allow a relatively risk-free intervention (though it could be argued that risk-taking is an unfortunate but unavoidable element of the profession of arms and of the exercise of foreign policy).

UDI produced inter- and intra-party political problems in Britain.[9] With a number of his more left-wing MPs demanding harsh and immediate action against the Smith regime, Harold Wilson found himself relying, to a considerable extent, on the Opposition for support over Rhodesia. At this time the Labour Party had a tiny majority in the House of Commons. In October 1964 it had a majority of five. On 7 November, four days before UDI, this had been reduced to one, and if the Wilson government had then lost both the pending by-elections it would have lost its absolute majority. Some commentators regard this political factor as a major influence on Wilson's handling of the crisis:

> One may leave aside the rather complex problem of adequate capability – a very limited quick military intervention at an early stage might well have toppled the regime on the basis of its appeal to the Southern Rhodesians' loyalty to the Crown. It seems clear that the occasion to use force in an action which was internationally demanded was abandoned owing to domestic pressures.[10]

Not only was the majority opinion in the House of Commons unsympathetic towards any prospect of military intervention, but public opinion in general, at the time of UDI, and soon thereafter, was not supportive of military intervention. A month before UDI a public opinion poll showed only 2 per cent favoured force in the event of Smith leading Rhodesia to independence without London's approval, 15 per cent were in favour of trade restrictions, 63 per cent were in favour of referring the matter to the United Nations and 18 per cent were in favour of no action at all. When asked where their sympathies lay, 29 per cent of the sample said with the Africans and 28 per cent said with the European Rhodesians.[11]

The Wilson government was well aware that the use of force, if not immediately successful, could be very damaging politically. The image of another Suez hung heavy over Wilson. As regards public opinion, Wilson's perception appears to have paid dividends. Following UDI a Gallup poll recorded 68 per cent in favour of Wilson's handling of the crisis, and such support never fell below 50 per cent.[12] Among the British public there was an apathy about an issue that, to the Southern Rhodesians of all races, was a political issue of direct vital interest. A third domestic factor weakening the case of British military intervention was the doubts and rumours concerning the enthusiasm of the British army for such a task, against a white population of predominantly British stock:

> British intervention would also have raised a ticklish problem of military loyalties. An enterprise designed to topple Smith so as to make Nkomo Prime Minister would not have proved popular with the British army, a force composed of professional soldiers not distinguished for the fervour of their anticolonial sentiments.[13]

There were rumours of possible resignations at a high level, notably Lord Mountbatten, Chief of Defence Staff, as well as lower-ranking officers, and there is no doubt that questions about the loyalty of the armed forces did weigh considerably on Whitehall decision-makers,[14] though it is difficult to ascertain how strong a factor it was in the decision not to intervene.

The second major factor influencing the Wilson government's decision was military and economic overstretch. At first glance, Britain's capabilities seemed more than adequate for the task. Britain's defence budget was 400 times that of Rhodesia's; it deployed 58,000 troops east of Suez, 62,000 in Germany, 23,000 in the Mediterranean area and 9,000 troops elsewhere in the world. Britain was one of the world's four nuclear military powers. In the House of Commons Jeremy Thorpe reflected the incredulity felt by many when he declared that 'it would be a fantastic position if this country were incapable of putting down a rebellion of a population the size of that of Portsmouth'.[15] Yet, as seen from Downing Street, this was the case. It was reckoned that to oust the Smith regime and police the country between 15,000 and 25,000 troops would be required, but there was no more than one brigade group (approximately 3,000–3,500 men)[16] available in the strategic reserve while, simultaneously, over 50,000 military personnel were engaged in Malaysia, where there were grave fears of escalation. British forces were also involved in peace-keeping in Cyprus and colonial policing in Aden. Indeed, forces had already been drawn from the British Army on the Rhine to contribute to these residual imperial and colonial duties and Britain's West European allies would not have looked kindly on further reductions for extra-North Atlantic duties of prolonged duration, particularly for an exercise not viewed as at all central to Western security. In the event of intervention one of the British units with a key role would have been the Special Air Service. However, it had a sister unit in the Rhodesian forces with which it had often exercised.

Perhaps the most formidable military problem was that of logistics. Rhodesia was land-locked, with sympathetic states, the Republic of South Africa and Portuguese Mozambique, to the south and east. The only favourable route to Southern Rhodesia over land was from Zambia, and Zambia would need to be supplied by air via the Tanzanian capital Dar es Salaam. To move one brigade group – and that was all that was available – 5,000 miles to Dar es Salaam would take well over a week and would have required the whole efforts of RAF Transport Command. Any larger forces would have meant the requisitioning of civilian aircraft. Furthermore, a base with fuel and repair depots would need to be set up in Zambia for which 'air support would be necessary at least to discourage interference by the small, not ultra-modern, but well-trained and determined Rhodesian air force'.[17] British capabilities, in terms of personnel and logistical support, were deemed to be inadequate to launch an operation within an acceptable level of risk.

Topography was very much on the side of the Rhodesians. Operating in their own country with internal lines of communication, the Rhodesian armed forces were mobile and encountered few logistical problems. Any British interventionary force other than a small paratroop drop (which may or may not have had the psychological effect of ending the rebellion, and if it had not the consequences would have been disastrous . . . ?) would have needed to cross the Zambian–Rhodesian border but there are only three main crossing points for conventional forces – the rest of the border being Lake Kariba, gorges, or escarpment.

Even in the event of British military intervention, British forces would have encountered a small but well-trained, well-led 'European' army which, on its home ground, would have been difficult to defeat *quickly*. Rhodesia was unique among British colonies in that it financed and developed its own security forces. The Rhodesian security forces in 1965 consisted of an SAS unit of about 150 paratroopers and a battalion of light infantry and ancillary units of engineers and signals. However, strength in depth in the Rhodesian (European) forces was to be found in the reserves. All residents between 18 and 23 years of age, other than African, were obliged to do four-and-a-half months' continuous military service, followed by three years' part-time training with an active territorial battalion. In 1965 four such battalions were immediately available for service with probably four more reserve battalions made up of men who had completed their regular military training. There was also a regular African battalion, with European officers. Very important, the police force in Rhodesia, composed of 2,000 Europeans and 4,000 Africans, was of the highest quality, with high morale. As a result, Salisbury did not identify internal security as a problem. The Rhodesian air force, many members of which were RAF trained, also had to be taken into account. It consisted of forty to fifty Vampire, Hunter and Canberra operational aircraft, a squadron of transports and some helicopters and light aircraft.

One important vital question posed was 'would the Rhodesians fight?'. If a stick of the Queen's paratroopers dropped on to Salisbury, would they be resisted, or would the Smith government collapse? Questions of loyalty and morale were very difficult to answer. Certainly, about 25 per cent of the Rhodesian armed forces were recruited directly from Britain, and there was a residual loyalty to the Crown. However, there was a strong tide of white nationalism, the majority of white Rhodesians felt they deserved independence, and the officer corps certainly reflected the mood of the Europeans in the country. There were few doubts as to the loyalty of the European police to the Smith regime and, as a precaution, just after UDI some African police units were disarmed. In 1964, the year before UDI, Smith had purged the high command of the army and air force, placing in charge commanders felt to be more sympathetic to UDI.

Faced by a strong, well-trained, apparently coherent military force over a political issue of great import to the Rhodesians but very distant from the bulk of the British population, and well aware of the immense logistical problems, the Wilson government did not intervene with military force. A short, sharp military operation might well have produced collapse, and perhaps other unforeseen consequences for which a large British military presence would have been required. Wilson had images of Suez to the forefront of his mind and, though there were some obvious asymmetries, there were also some parallels, and Wilson wished to avoid such an entanglement. Britain simply did not have the capabilities, nor was there the unanimous public support, to *ensure* success.

In addition to the risk of military failure or stalemate, and political storms at home, the British economy was in a delicate state. An £800m. balance-of-payments deficit was expected for the financial year 1964/5, and further military adventures in the developing world would have increased the strain.

In the broader international context there was the fear, especially in view of the earlier troubles in the Congo, of the escalation and spill-over potential of a military blow-up in Southern Rhodesia. This fear was illustrated by Britain's behaviour in the United Nations in December 1966 when oil was included in sanctions. George Brown made it clear that Britain would resist any proposal which would commit the United Nations to taking action against South Africa or Portugal for refusing to comply with economic sanctions against the illegal Rhodesian regime. The last thing Britain wanted was a UN peace-keeping force, including Soviet or East European forces, operating in Southern Africa:

> To a Britain that had been disturbed by the prospect of Russian intervention in the Congo imbroglio four and five years before, this was not idle speculation. In any case, even if the Russians did not participate there still might be an OAU army or substantial African contingents in a UN force; in addition, Rhodesian nationalists might set up 'governments-in-exile' and be recognised by some African states, in and out of the Commonwealth, although not by Britain. It did not take much imagination to think that Rhodesia, if mishandled, could 'set Africa ablaze', as the point was sometimes emotionally put.[18]

Military non-intervention was very poor for Britain's international image, nowhere more so than in the developing world, the area where most of the contemporary security problems were perceived to be located. However, the British decision not to intervene militarily to displace the Smith regime in Salisbury was an accurate reflection of Britain's declining military and economic capability to project meaningful, sustained military power beyond the North Atlantic. The decision had been taken in 1965 to evacuate Aden, come what may, by 1968, and the end of Confrontation in Malaysia was greeted with considerable relief the following year. To have undertaken a major military operation 5,000 miles from home in late 1965 or early 1966, in addition to commitments elsewhere, would have belied the reality of Britain's military position.

Wilson's wise decision not to intervene in Rhodesia with military force in

1965/6 ended a decade of successful but very risky British military intervention. Other instruments for the projection of power and influence had to be adopted. In the case of Rhodesia, none too successfully, it was economic sanctions. In the Nigerian Civil War Britain relied upon military aid and sales to exert influence on the federal government, and in the case of the Vietnam War historical and diplomatic influence derived from the 'Special Relationship'. Indeed, the Nigerian Civil War and the Vietnam War were instances of crises of international security in the extra-North Atlantic world before the end of the 1960s which Britain, by the rationales and criteria of the supporters of Britain's global rule, ought to have had a major, if not military, role in managing. In both cases it was out of the question. In the Nigerian case there was never an invitation from the federal government to intervene and even if there had been Britain did not have the military capabilities, in 1967, to intervene on the scale required. Furthermore, it is extremely doubtful if there would have been the necessary parliamentary and public support in view of the competent Biafran propaganda campaigns. During the Vietnam War there were occasional suggestions from President Johnson from 1964 onwards[19] for token British military contributions but Wilson, either in the midst of Confrontation or winding down, had no intention of sending British forces to Vietnam. The evident dangers of escalation, British military overstretch, domestic economic problems and, of course, the domestic political furore it would have produced, not least in the Labour Party itself, were ample reasons for avoiding any more South-East Asian military commitments. By the late 1960s, reflecting changes in the international system such as the Sino-Soviet rift, anti-communism and perceptions of the Chinese threat were no longer fears sufficient to produce nearly unanimous support for military interventions outside the NATO area.

By 1970, following the defence retrenchments of the 1960s, and illustrated by, most significantly, the Rhodesian crisis and, less significantly, the Nigerian Civil War and the Vietnam War, Britain had clearly abandoned any real pretence, despite the very limited, consultative Five Power Defence Agreement in South-East Asia,[20] of global military status. As all British Defence White Papers since 1967 had declared, Britain would concentrate its military power in the North Atlantic area, and become a Eurocentric military power. However, in 1974 a crisis erupted in which Britain was directly involved, not only through historical connections but by international treaty and the presence of forces at the heart of the crisis, which raised grave doubts as to the capability and propensity of Britain even to project military power in the geo-political area prescribed by the North Atlantic Treaty.

The Cyprus Crisis of 1974

Tension had been rising in the Eastern Mediterranean since the early summer of 1974 over a dispute between the Greek and Turkish governments about oil-prospecting rights in the Aegean Sea. In addition to truculent language between Greece and Turkey over natural resources, Greece, ruled by an authoritarian military junta since 1967, adopted an increasingly hostile posture towards the Makarios government of Cyprus in Nicosia. This reached such a pitch that it caused dissent in the Greek cabinet, and the Greek foreign minister resigned over the policy.

Poor relations between the Greek military government and Makarios plummeted even further when he published the content of a letter he sent to the Greek president, General Gizikis, in which he accused Greek officers in the Cypriot National Guard of allying with EOKA−B terrorists to plot his overthrow. He demanded the withdrawal of nearly 650 Greek officers in the Cypriot National Guard. Makarios's suspicions and fears were vindicated when the National Guard overthrew his government on 15 July and installed a former EOKA terrorist, Nikos Sampson, as the new president of Cyprus. Despite claims to the contrary Makarios escaped the attempts to assassinate him, was rescued from the Paphos area by a British helicopter and taken to the British military base at Episkopi, and thence to London to request British intervention.

However, despite a plea from a legitimate Commonwealth government which Britain continued to recognise, despite legitimisation of any British military intervention by Article IV of the 1960 Treaty of Guarantee to which Britain was a co-signatory, despite the presence of British forces at the heart of the crisis, despite near-certain international public approval, despite the attraction of interposing a third party between two hostile NATO allies, Britain declined to intervene. The Wilson government, strongly advised by James Callaghan, the Foreign Secretary, decided to rely upon diplomatic pressure to resolve the crisis.

Two opportunities for intervention presented themselves: the first, immediately after the Makarios government was overthrown and the second when, in the face of British inactivity and the rejection of a Turkish proposal made in London by the Turkish prime minister, Bulent Ecevit,[21] of joint Turkish-British intervention to safeguard the sovereignty of Cyprus and keep the peace, Turkey intervened alone. Prior to the Turkish intervention Callaghan called upon Greece to remove the Greek National Guard officers from Cyprus, and to send a representative to urgent trilateral talks in London between Greece, Turkey and Britain. By this time the United States was taking a rather belated interest in the conflict between two of its south-east European allies, and the Assistant Secretary of State, Joseph Sisco, arrived in Europe to help Callaghan find his non-military solution to the crisis.[22] In search of a diplomatic solution Sisco visited both Athens and Ankara.

Faced with *de facto* Enosis (the union of Greece and Cyprus – the long-term goal of EOKA), Turkey launched a small-scale military intervention in the Kyrenia region of the island on 20 July. Geography gave Turkey an enormous advantage in any dispute with Greece over Cyprus. Although the majority of the Cypriot population are of Greek descent, Cyprus is a mere 40 miles from Turkey but over 300 miles from the Greek mainland. Greece and Turkey both mobilised, but fighting was limited to the island of Cyprus. The Cypriot National Guard was composed of 12,000 conscripts with 650 Greek officers and equipped with 32 tanks.[23] The political result of the none-too-inspiring Turkish intervention – slow progress was made by the limited, somewhat complacent Turkish forces, surprised at the quality of Greek Cypriot resistance – was that Sampson was replaced by Glafkos Clerides, Speaker of the Cypriot House of Representatives and constitutional head of state in the absence of Makarios. The Greek military junta in Athens, surprised and panicked by Ankara's bellicose reaction, collapsed, and Greece returned to civilian rule on 23 July.

A ceasefire was agreed on 22 July but Nicosia, the major objective of the Turkish forces, was not taken, and half the Turkish-Cypriot population was still in areas controlled by the Greek Cypriots, though the Greek Cypriots in the newly occupied Turkish areas acted as potential bargaining counters.

Between 23 July and 14 August two conferences, chaired by Callaghan and supported by the United States, were held in Geneva in an attempt to solve the crisis through diplomacy rather than force. Although Britain tried to act as an honest broker between Greece and Turkey the conferences were unsuccessful. During the ceasefire period the Turkish army had increased its numbers to 40,000 troops and about 200 tanks. Faced by Greek reluctance to accept Turkish proposals for 'a cantonal division of the island between the two ethnic groups under a federal government of limited authority',[24] Turkish forces took the offensive on 14 August. More crossed over from Turkey and by 16 August northern Cyprus beyond the 'Attila line', which ran from Famagusta through Nicosia to Kokkina, was under the authority of the Turkish army.

This second phase of the Turkish invasion resulted in Greece leaving the integrated military infrastructure of NATO, diplomatic deadlock over a divided island, Turkish control of 40 per cent of Cyprus (a Commonwealth country), a third of the Greek-Cypriot population being made refugees, heavy casualties, and considerable devastation to the Cypriot tourist and agricultural industries from which the island is still recovering.

Britain's military role in the Cyprus tragedy was minimal. Tourists caught in the crisis were efficiently evacuated, and the Sovereign Base Areas were reinforced for their own protection and as havens for refugees from the inter-communal atrocities. In the autumn of 1974 one commentator declared: 'As the Cyprus situation moves towards deadlock it is increasingly apparent that only a much more robust British interpretation of her rights and obligations under the 1960 Treaty of Guarantee could have averted the present situation, which is likely to fester for the indefinite future.'[25]

Hence, the question arises, 'why did Britain not intervene militarily but instead resort to diplomatic means?'; and the supplementary question which arises is, 'what does this say about British military power, even in the European theatre?'

There were two major sets of reasons why Britain did not undertake military intervention in Cyprus in July 1974 – political and military. First, one of the primary political reasons was that Sampson's *coup* meant the final demise of the 1960 Treaty of London arrangements which had established Cypriot independence. The constitution established by that treaty had not been working at all properly since the inter-communal troubles of 1963–4 which had necessitated British military intervention, first alone, and then later as part of the United Nations peace-keeping force. It would have been nonsensical for Britain to intervene to restore an essentially non-working constitution. Inter-communal talks had been stumbling along since 1964 and, it has been reported,[26] there was a strong feeling in the Foreign Office that, to a considerable extent, the Greek Cypriots had brought many of their problems upon themselves. To have accompanied Turkey in an intervention was politically impossible – Britain and Turkey would have had different objectives. Britain's objective would have been, if not to restore Makarios, at least to safeguard the integrity of the state of Cyprus and produce a new constitution. On the other hand, Ankara had no intention of restoring Makarios, and its primary objective was to safeguard the Turkish Cypriots. The end-result of Turkish intervention was the division of the island, a result in which Britain could not have participated and could never have concurred. In addition, Turkish intervention had the effect of uniting many of the Greek-Cypriot factions. British participation would have brought near-unanimous opposition from the Greek-Cypriot community, both pro-Enosis and pro-Makarios.

Though the government was strongly criticised by a House of Commons Select Committee Report[27] for not intervening with military force, Britain's available military capabilities were clearly not up to the task of achieving the desired British political objectives. British forces were on the island and in the two Sovereign Base Areas, but of the 8,000 to hand most were concerned with the management and control of the airfields and with logistics, with only about 2,600 actually trained and equipped for combat.[28] There were no British tanks or ground-attack aircraft on the island. As experienced in 1963/4, it takes more than a few thousand troops to keep the peace successfully. If Britain had tried to intervene in 1974 with just over 3,000 troops (900 Royal Marines were in HMS *Hermes*, somewhere in the Mediterranean) and found itself attempting to keep the peace between 12,000 Cypriot National Guards and over 40,000 Turkish troops the consequences would have been disastrous. Britain's military air-lift capability was incapable of rushing adequate forces to the Sovereign Base Area airfields quickly enough, and the Chief of the Defence Staff, Sir Michael Carver, argued strongly against intervention.[29] The Cabinet had little hesitation in accepting his advice.

A squadron of ground-attack Phantoms was dispatched from Britain during the crisis but this was an effort to deter the Turkish army from attempting to capture Nicosia airport. Throughout the crisis the airport was in United Nations hands, which included British contingents, with orders to fight if attacked. Appalled at the prospect of needless British deaths in the face of Turkish tanks, the Wilson government sent the Phantoms as an indication of British concern over the status of the airport. It is interesting to note that the back-up equipment for the Phantoms' anti-tank role could not be air-lifted to Cyprus in time for its possible use. Nevertheless, Wilson did succeed in persuading Ecevit to stop Turkish forces on the airfield's northern perimeter.

In the circumstances, the decision by the British government to eschew the military intervention option appears to have been prudent. The 1960 constitution was beyond salvation, and the political objective of any military intervention, beyond saving lives and keeping the peace, was unclear and problematical – all the more so in the event of Turkish military intervention. There was also the distinct possibility that British actions would have strongly displeased both sides in the dispute, and this would merely have further complicated an already complex and delicate situation. However, more significantly, even if the British government had wished to intervene militarily in a crisis in the European theatre *not* involving the major East–West powers the required military capabilities and logistics support were absent.

British military non-intervention in the Cyprus crisis of 1974 suggests that even before the 1975 Defence Review Britain had not merely withdrawn from east of Suez as a military power of consequence but had become a north-west Eurocentric military power, not just Eurocentric. The Defence Review of 1975 emphasised the reality of this status, accelerated the process and appeared to prescribe the geo-political limits of British military power for the foreseeable future.

Notes: Chapter 5

1 Henry Fairlie, *The Kennedy Promise* (London: Eyre Methuen, 1973), p. 293.
2 See J. D. B. Miller, *Survey of Commonwealth Affairs, Problems of Expansion and Attrition 1953–1969* (London: Oxford University Press, 1974), p. 168.
3 See Kenneth Young, *Rhodesia and Independence* (London: Dent, 1976), p. 319.
4 John Day, 'A failure of foreign policy: the case of Rhodesia', in Michael Leifer (ed.), *Constraints and Adjustments in British Foreign Policy* (London: Allen & Unwin, 1972), p. 152.
5 See Peter Harris, *Studies in African Politics* (London: Hutchinson, 1970), p. 136.
6 See Day, op. cit., p. 155.
7 *House of Commons Debates*, 1 November 1965, quoted in Miller, op. cit., pp. 208–9.
8 See Robert C. Good, *UDI. The International Politics of the Rhodesian Rebellion* (London: Faber, 1973), p. 18.
9 ibid., p. 61, and also Joseph Frankel, *British Foreign Policy 1965–1973* (London: Oxford University Press, 1975), p. 137.
10 Frankel, op. cit.
11 Miller, op. cit., p. 212.
12 See Good, op. cit., p. 63.
13 Lewis H. Gann, *Central Africa. The Former British States* (Englewood Cliffs, NJ: Prentice-Hall, 1971), p. 158.

14 Confidential discussion with a retired senior civil servant.
15 Quoted in Good, op. cit., pp. 55–6.
16 See William Gutteridge, 'Rhodesia: the use of military force', *The World Today*, vol. 21, no. 12 (1965), p. 499.
17 ibid., p. 500.
18 Miller, op. cit., p. 211.
19 See Harold Wilson, *The Labour Government 1964–1970. A Personal Record* (London: Weidenfeld & Nicolson, 1970), pp. 18, 48 and 264.
20 See Frankel, op. cit., p. 129.
21 See Peter Kellner and Christopher Hitchens, *Callaghan. The Road to Number Ten* (London: Cassell, 1976), p. 138.
22 See Richard Clogg, 'Greece and the Cyprus crisis', *The World Today*, vol. 30, no. 9 (1974), p. 365.
23 See 'The Cyprus crisis', *Strategic Survey 1974* (London: IISS, 1975), p. 77.
24 ibid., p. 79.
25 Clogg, op. cit., p. 368.
26 See 'Cyprus: what could Britain have done?', *Sunday Times*, 23 May 1976, p. 6.
27 See *The Select Committee on Cyprus, Minutes of Evidence, Thursday, 19 February, 1976* (London: HMSO, 1976).
28 See *The Economist*, 20 July 1974, p. 26.
29 *Sunday Times*, op. cit.

6 Since 1974

Contraction of Capabilities

The year 1974 not only witnessed the marked inability of Britain to project major military force in faraway corners of the European theatre, but saw the Labour government initiate a review of British defence policy which would, *inter alia*, restrict even further British capabilities to pursue a military role on the European flanks of the NATO area. Yet only four years before, in the midst of withdrawal from east of Suez, considerable importance had been attached to and pride derived from the contribution Britain could make to the security of NATO's vulnerable flanks:

> Our sea, land and air forces make a significant contribution to the defence of the flanks of NATO. The United Kingdom Mobile Force, consisting of elements of the Army Strategic Command and Royal Air Force Support Command, provides a capability for rapid reinforcement from the United Kingdom. The Army and the Royal Air Force contribute to the Allied Command Europe Mobile Force which can be used on either flank. In addition one Royal Marine Commando Group has a reinforcement role on the Northern Flank for which it is being equipped for warfare in very cold climates. In the Mediterranean, a naval amphibious force which formed part of our increased naval presence in 1969, will be increased again this year. Her Majesty's ships, air forces and Royal Marine Commando units have taken part in major NATO exercises in the Mediterranean in the past year.[1]

But by 1974 this compensatory role for the British armed forces, only recently obliged to abandon historic tramping-grounds outside Europe, came under scrutiny, and the apparently irreversible decline in intervention capabilities continued.

In the Defence White Paper published in 1975,[2] in an effort to reduce defence spending as a proportion of the gross national product from an annual figure of $5\frac{1}{2}$ to $4\frac{1}{2}$ per cent and to save £4,700 million over the following ten years, certain extra-North Atlantic commitments were 'tidied up' but in the NATO area the British capabilities to project military force to the flanks, especially the southern flank, bore the brunt of the savings. The principal reductions in commitments and capabilities were as follows:

(i) after 1976 no British maritime forces were to be committed to the Mediterranean in support of NATO;

(ii)   British forces were no longer declared to CENTO;
(iii) British forces in Cyprus were to be reduced;
(iv)   British forces were to be withdrawn from Malta by 1979;
(v)   the Hong Kong garrison was to be reduced;
(vi)   withdrawal from Gan and Mauritius was to be completed by April 1976;
(vii) subject to consultation with the Sultan of Brunei, a Gurkha battalion was to be withdrawn from Brunei;
(viii) no British forces were to be committed to the Five Power Defence Agreement except a small contribution to the Integrated Air Defence System;
(ix)   the Simonstown base agreement with the Republic of South Africa was ended;
(x)   the permanent deployment of two Royal Navy frigates to the Caribbean would cease in 1976.

Complementary to the reduction of the British Mediterranean NATO forces and the rationalisation of commitments and forces outside the European theatre, the Defence Review of 1975 proposed reductions in the specialised reinforcement forces for NATO – force elements of which had been lauded in the 1960s as making a unique contribution to Britain's capabilities rapidly to project military force outside the NATO area, and in the years before 1975, to peripheral areas of NATO Europe (see Table 6.1).

In response to Allied pressure some minor adjustments were made to the Defence Review's proposals, but the end result of the exercise was, at some financial saving, to weaken further Britain's long-range military force projection capabilities. The exercise of British military force in any sustained and major manner was to be confined to north-west Europe and the North Atlantic. As one commentary noted soon after publication of the Defence Review:

> All this takes one stage further the concentration of the British defence effort in NATO Europe, which was a major trend of the decisions of January 1968. But to this is now added a withdrawal from some part of the commitments to the flanks of NATO, missions for which both the Mobile Force and the Royal Marine Commandos were equipped and trained.[3]

In the 1970s the commitment to the defence of NATO Europe, particularly continental north-west Europe and the eastern Atlantic approaches, became the focus of British defence policy. By 1977 non-NATO defence commitments were accounting for less than 1.5 per cent of the defence budget in contrast to a figure of around 20 per cent in the mid-1960s.[4] Such total commitment to NATO obligations performs not only a defence function but also a most important diplomatic function, demonstrating British support of the Alliance and profound concern over the security of continental

Table 6.1 *Proposed Reductions in Specialised Reinforcement Forces for NATO*

Before Review	After Review
(A) ACE mobile force (UK contribution)	No change
1 Land Element	
one battalion group	
+ force troops	
2 Air element	
one Harrier squadron	
four Wessex helicopters	
+ communications and control units	
(B) UK mobile force	
1 Land Element	Reduced to:
three air-portable brigades	one air-portable brigade group
+ divisional troops	(larger and heavier)
+ logistic support force	+ support and logistic force
2 Air Element	
three Phantom/Jaguar squadrons	Same, less Andover squadron
three Wessex/Puma squadrons	
one Andover squadron	
(C) UK joint airborne task force	Abandoned
Headquarters	Limited parachute capability
Parachute Force (two battalions	required
+ support)	
Air Transport Force (five Hercules	
squadrons)	
(D) Amphibious force	Reduced to:
Royal Marines brigade headquarters	Royal Marines brigade
	headquarters
+ four commando groups (one	+ three commandos (one
mountain and arctic trained)	mountain and arctic trained)
+ logistic regiment	+ logistic regiment
+ army support units	+ army support units
two RN Wessex helicopter squadrons	one RN Wessex helicopter
	squadron
two commando ships	HMS *Hermes* in a secondary
	role as a commando ship
two assault ships	two assault ships (one in reserve)
afloat support	afloat support

Source: Statement in Defence Estimates 1975, Cmnd 5976 (London: HMSO, 1975), ch. 1, p. 12.

West Europe. In this regard the British Army of the Rhine (BAOR) is acknowledged to perform a vital role, especially in view of the long tradition of British military non-involvement on the Continent in peacetime.[5] Obviously the major function of BAOR is military, as part of the conventional deterrence and defence forces assigned to the Atlantic Alliance, but under the London and Paris Agreements of October 1954 Britain is obliged to maintain four divisions and a tactical air force on the European mainland until 1998. This facilitated the entry of the Federal German Republic into NATO in 1955 by helping to allay the historic fears of a re-militarised Germany held by the Federal Republic's close West European neighbours. The agreements do allow the withdrawal of BAOR before 1998 in the event of either 'an acute overseas emergency' or 'too great a strain on the external finances of the United Kingdom'. The latter contingency now seems the most likely, but given the diplomatic repercussions, not least from the Soviet Union which could fear an expansion of the Bundeswehr to compensate for the loss of BAOR in NATO's forward defence, and the reality of the cost of redundancy payments and housing BAOR in Britain, the likely financial savings do not seem proportionate to the political costs incurred by withdrawal.

The policy of the Conservative government in 1981 to sustain Britain's European land and air contributions and to rationalise instead the RN surface fleet demonstrated support for Britain's continental commitment to NATO.[6] The naval cuts envisaged by the 1981 Defence Review suggest that the Thatcher administration continues to attach the highest importance to deterrence on the Central Front at the cost of power-projection capabilities on the high seas. However, the government is still loath to accept the abandonment of any interventionary role and, as will be discussed in Chapter 7, some limited means are devoted to facilitating intervention if the need should arise. 'Flexibility' has become the key military concept in British defence policy in the 1980s, with the notion of sections of the Eurocentric British armed services being able to fulfil out-of-area tasks if required.

Continuing Commitments

Including the internal security problem of Ulster[7] (costing the defence budget over £65 million a year by 1977, and entailing at least a quadrupling of the 1969 garrison number of 3,000 troops), the Atlantic–Channel naval role, the commitment to European defence on the Continent, the ground and air defence of the British homeland and the maintenance of the strategic nuclear deterrent will continue, in some configuration, to be the foci of British defence policy throughout the 1980s. Unease and disagreement over the character and longevity of this balance of commitment and forces has been created by doubts about the capability of future defence budgets to support the major Alliance roles described above and simultaneously to procure a replacement for the Polaris SSBN strategic deterrent.[8] Against the backdrop of considerable informed debate among the 'foreign policy public', and amid some stark and dramatic scenarios,[9] the Conservative government has insisted that, with a rationalisation of defence spending and a better balanced arms procurement policy, the £7 billion or £8 billion (at 1981 prices) required to procure the Trident SSBN system over a ten-year period can be managed.

The Falklands conflict of 1982 merely exacerbated this debate. Further uncertainty has been created over resources available for future defence requirements, given the replacement costs of material lost in the campaign and also the costs of sustaining a credible deterrent against any future Argentinian aggression. In addition, various interested parties have used the Falklands experience to support arguments about the utility of conventional forces, and a preference for particular types of conventional forces, not conducive to the resolution of the Trident debate.[10] In this regard, one major result of the Falklands War is that the carrier HMS *Invincible*, earmarked to be sold to Australia, is now being retained, and the front-line surface strength of the RN sustained at fifty-five – five above the official figure proposed in 1981. However, this slight reprieve for the RN does not signal any major revision of strategy, but the necessity to service heightened commitments in the South Atlantic.

Since Confrontation, and apart from the Falklands War, the use of British military force in the extra-North Atlantic world has been limited to three different types of operations – colonial policing as in Anguilla and the New Hebrides, limited deterrence as in Belize and the low-intensity, low profile 'secret' wars in the Gulf states where British officers and men assist indigenous forces fighting communist-supported insurgents. The first two types do not really fall into the intervention category. Neither Anguilla nor the New Hebrides was fully sovereign or belonged to a fully sovereign state. Britain was responsible for the defence and diplomatic relations of the Caribbean state of St Kitts, Nevis and Anguilla,[11] from which Anguilla was threatening to secede in 1969. Fearing criminal influences on the small Caribbean island, the Wilson government dispatched a small combined force of troops and Metropolitan police. The arrival of these forces calmed the situation, and allowed a constitutional solution to the dispute to be worked out. Similarly, over a decade later, the group of islands in the South Pacific known as the New Hebrides, where the presence of British troops was required, was not a fully sovereign state but a colonial condominium under the joint protection of Britain and France. Independence for the New Hebrides, under the new name of Vanuata, had been set for May 1980 but owing to internal political upheavals was postponed until the end of July 1980. A secessionist movement on one of the major islands, Espiritu Santu, supported by French settlers and American 'Libertarian' businessmen seeking a tax haven, threatened the political and territorial integrity of the new nation, and Canberra and Wellington put pressure on London and Paris to end the rebellion. Despite agreements to co-operate, small British (one rifle company of 42 Royal Marine Commando) and French forces arrived at the New Hebrides to the sound of Anglo-French bickering and confusion over what appropriate action should be taken. A French settlers' lobby had begun to gain influence in Paris, and London was reluctant to use force against French settlers without the whole-hearted support of Paris. None the less, the rebellion was contained until 200 troops from Papua New Guinea arrived in August and put an end to the affair with minimum bloodshed. British and French forces withdrew in August, and the Papua New Guinea forces withdrew in September.[12]

British forces in Belize (formerly British Honduras) number over 1,500, and fulfil a deterrent function against the invasion threat that is inherent in Guatemala's 150-year-old territorial claim to the former self-governing colony. The Belizeans are fortunate in that the weight of international public opinion is on their side, with the United Nations General Assembly voting 139 to 0 in November 1979 in favour of Belize's independence and sovereignty.[13] This was the first time the United States openly and directly opposed Guatemala over this issue. In March 1981, after negotiations in London, and much to Britain's relief, Guatemala renounced its claim to Belize. The quid pro quo for Guatemala was that it would have use of facilities at Belize's sea ports, it would be allowed to build two oil pipelines across Belize, and would share the use of some uninhabited cays (islets and reefs) east of Belize's southernmost coast. Belize was to restrict territorial waters to 3 miles in the area of the cays, which would leave a clear sea corridor into the Caribbean for Guatemala. Joint offshore oil exploration was also envisaged – an enterprise oil companies had been reluctant to tackle so long as the Guatemalan threat persisted.[14]

Unfortunately negotiations in May and July 1981 over details of the March agreement were not successful, and led to a reassertion of the Guatemalan claim. As a consequence, and despite the independence of Belize in September 1981, the British military presence continues for an unspecified period, at an annual cost to the British taxpayer of at least £25 million. British governments have been anxious to relinquish this Central American commitment as soon as possible, but the Guatemalan population is forty times the size of that of Belize, and the indigenous Belizean defence forces number less than 700 and are poorly equipped and trained. Efforts are being made to improve the Belizean defence forces, but given the Falklands experience it is unlikely that there will be a precipitous move to abandon the commitment to the defence of Belize in the face of irredentist claims from a bellicose Latin American dictatorship.[15]

Since the decade of interventions following Suez the use of British military force most akin to the military intervention of those years has taken place in the Gulf state of Oman, in the low-intensity warfare against anti-royalist, communist-supported rebels. This type of assistance has proved most cost-effective and successful in the support of a friendly government of a modernising pro-Western state in a volatile but strategically important region of the world, contiguous with the vulnerable, oil-rich sheikhdoms on the southern shores of the Gulf and overlooking the Strait of Hormuz.

The end of 1971 saw the military withdrawal of Britain from the Gulf, a region where it had maintained an equilibrium for over a hundred years. The impending British withdrawal formed the backdrop for an upsurge of

Sino-Soviet competition in southern Arabia, and the escalation of an initially Chinese-sponsored rebellion in the Dhofar province of Oman, receiving succour and aid from the increasingly Marxist state of South Yemen (formerly Aden and the South Arabian Federation until the British withdrawal in 1968).[16] Until the overthrow of the reactionary Sultan Said bin Taimur by his son Qaboos in July 1970 the war went badly for the Omani government. The modernising and relatively more liberal Qaboos quickly increased the size and sophistication of his armed forces and gradually drove back the Popular Front for the Liberation of Oman and the Arabian Gulf (PFLOAG). Notable features of the long campaign were the large contingent of British officers and men on secondment to the sultan's forces or employed under contract, and the military aid and advice received not only from Britain but also from Jordan and Iran. Indeed, an Iranian brigade of 3,500 men assisted on operations in Dhofar. By 1975 the final South Yemeni forces were driven across the border, leaving only isolated pockets of rebels in the eastern mountains of Dhofar.[17]

Dhofar is a persistent problem in that it is isolated from the rest of Oman by several hundred miles of desert and the indigenous people are closer ethnographically to south Arabians than the Gulf Arabs in north Oman, while some of the mountain tribes speak languages other than Arabic which are incomprehensible even to other Arabs. In an attempt to decrease the sense of separation and uniqueness Sultan Qaboos has devoted considerable resources to health, educational, agricultural, transport and irrigation development since 1970.[18]

The counter-insurgency campaign in Oman was declared at an end in December 1975. Over 700 British nationals participated in the campaign. A unit of the Special Air Service undertook particularly dangerous work in training and leading local tribesmen, often former rebels, who joined the sultan's forces. The sultan's coastal navy trained under British direction, while a large number of regular British officers trained and commanded other elements of the sultan's forces and protected the airfield at Sallalah. There was also about 200 contract personnel who enlisted in Oman at the end of military careers in the British forces. Since 1975 a policy of 'Omanisation' has been under way, with strong British support, but it is a very slow process and a substantial, though low profile, British presence remains. In 1981, 130 officers were on secondment from Britain to the sultan's forces, and over 500 ex-servicemen from Britain were on contract in the Omani forces.[19] An SAS company is still operating in Dhofar against small groups of anti-sultan guerrillas.[20] With the Sultan of Oman paying all the bills, and the neighbouring pro-Western states discreetly supporting such a modest, low profile British presence, the Oman experience may serve as a model for how and when British forces ought to be used to support foreign policy objectives in the developing world, assuming an appropriate political environment.

The 'Old' Commonwealth no longer looks to Britain for defence provision in the manner expected in the imperial years between the world wars. Notice that this was no longer the case was given early in the postwar period when, in 1951, Australia and New Zealand preferred an alliance arrangement with the United States rather than with Britain. The subsequent ANZUS Pact did not include Britain, despite a ministerial statement in London that Britain wished to be included. The Second World War in the Far East had illustrated the woeful inadequacy of Britain to protect the dominions in that region, and Australia and New Zealand had to depend upon the United States for their defence. The withdrawal of Britain from India and the obvious debilitating effect of the war on British power strengthened the case for a security arrangement[21] with the United States rather than with Britain. The notion of the Commonwealth was no longer central to the defence and diplomatic concerns of the older dominions, and this feeling grew as the Second World War receded further into the past:

> Canada has used the Commonwealth as a means of fashioning a role and exerting influence, and as part of the search for a foreign policy that 'united us most'. By the end of the 1960s this emphasis was diminishing. Australia and New Zealand had been glad to assume the Commonwealth mantle in their joint military operations with Britain during the Malayan emergency but this . . . was something of a cloak for designs which were South East Asian rather than Commonwealth. Otherwise, apart from continuing their military interest in Malaysia and Singapore, they had found the association a source of embarrassment and disappointment in those critical aspects which involved Africa, although its social and traditional elements continued to influence them.[22]

In a similar vein the 'New' Commonwealth no longer looks to Britain for defence. India, despite the lingering British traditions in the armed services, has its own defence arrangements and, as experienced in the Indian-Chinese conflicts of the early 1960s, British sympathy is of little direct security benefit. Nigeria, the major military power in Black Africa, quickly abrogated an Anglo-Nigerian defence treaty soon after independence in October 1960. Contemporary Nigeria, militarily strong and possessing considerable natural resource power, has little need of British protection. In Black Africa in particular, continuing overt defence arrangements with the former metropole are seen by the ex-British colonies as conveying the image of neo-imperialism and hence, if anything, creating a target for domestic resentment rather than national reassurance. Outside the European theatre (not forgetting a brigade in West Berlin and smaller forces in Gibraltar and Cyprus) there are very few continuing British colonial or post-colonial commitments requiring or obliging defence. Such forces as there are in the last outposts of Empire perform 'possession', limited-deterrent, policing, or technical functions, as opposed to grand strategic functions.[23]

In Belize, performing a deterrent function, there is one armed reconnaissance troop, one artillery battery, one light AD troop, one engineer squadron, one infantry battalion, another infantry battalion (incomplete) and one flight of the Army Air Corps. There are also Harriers, Pumas and half a squadron of the RAF Regiment in the colony. A Royal Navy frigate is also available for the colony's defence. It is acknowledged that Hong Kong would be indefensible if an attack were launched from the People's Republic of China. Such an attack is improbable, and the British forces in Hong Kong perform a policing and immigration control function. The resident forces are composed of one UK infantry battalion, four Gurkha infantry battalions, a Gurkha engineer regiment, a squadron of Army Scout helicopters, five Royal Navy patrol craft and a squadron of Wessex RAF helicopters. Periodically reinforcements are sent to the colony to cope with upsurges in illegal immigration into the overcrowded colony, usually from the People's Republic of China. In 1979 an extra infantry battalion (later replaced by a Royal Marine commando), two Gurkha companies, three Army Scout helicopters and two Royal Navy Sea King helicopters were sent to reinforce the resident forces. Also in the Far East, Britain is supporting a Gurkha battalion in the sultanate of Brunei until 1983, when Britain will relinquish responsibility for Brunei's external affairs and its consultative commitment to Brunei's security. A naval unit performing technical duties is stationed on Diego Garcia, a British Indian Ocean island, to be used as a major staging post and a communications centre by the United States in its Rapid Deployment Force plans. The island's runways are being extended to take B-52 bombers, and its port facilities considerably improved. Belize and the Falkland Islands are the only places where British forces are performing a classical defence role beyond the North Atlantic.

The Falklands Episode

On 2 April 1982 Argentina invaded and occupied the British colony of the Falkland Islands. The response of the Conservative government, supported by an angry House of Commons, was to dispatch an impressive combined services task force with the objective of liberating the colony, if necessary by resorting to military force. By 5 April the first warships, the carriers HMS *Invincible* and *Hermes*, left Portsmouth on the 8,000-mile journey to the Falklands. In an admirable feat of organisation the task force, augmented by requisitioned and suitably converted merchant vessels and other warships, arrived at Ascension Island – halfway to the Falkland Islands – on 18 April. By the end of April the task force was in a position to attempt to impose not only a 200-mile maritime exclusion zone around the islands, which had been in force since 12 April based on the threat from British submarines, but a total exclusion zone implemented by seaborne air power as well as naval power. Nine thousand British troops with the task force posed the threat of major land battles if diplomatic efforts to resolve the dispute did not succeed. With the apparent failure of diplomatic moves to persuade the Argentinian government to withdraw its forces, eventually numbering about 12,000, the

British were obliged to land on the islands. On 14 June, following a success-ful but bloody campaign onshore, Argentinian forces on the Falklands surrendered.

The Falklands campaign of April–June 1982 was not military interven-tion, but rather the liberation and reoccupation of sovereign territory. As a result, some of the salient problems encountered in military intervention were either absent or considerably diminished. For example, as the Falkland Islands are British sovereign territory the legitimacy of British action was not seriously in question – though whether or not it is always prudent for a state to do what it is entitled to do when attempting to conduct sensitive foreign policy is another matter. Also, as military force was being used to liberate 'British' people and salvage British honour, the problem of adverse domestic public opinion was much less of a constraint, especially if a relatively short, sharp campaign with an acceptable level of casualties was the outcome. In the contemporary world of near-instant media coverage of international conflict, sustaining public support for limited wars can be a considerable problem for a democratic government. The geo-strategic location of the Falklands facilita-ted regulation of the news flow through the control of transmissions back to Britain.[24] It is difficult to imagine a conflict anywhere else in the world where such a tight rein on the media could have been implemented.

Nevertheless, this campaign does provide a contemporary illustration of the projection of military force to faraway places by a medium-rank West European power, and though not strictly falling under the aegis of military intervention does deserve consideration. This is particularly so as certain sec-tors of the British political and defence establishment have attempted to use the 'lessons' of the Falklands War, as they perceive them, to restructure aspects of British defence policy so as to facilitate the projection of military force outside the North Atlantic area.[25] Interests in defence of which British long-range power projection is required are rarely made clear by the support-ers of a redirected defence effort. Whatever notion of threat exists, it usually involves some scenario where Soviet and/or Cuban forces are challenging Western economic and political interests in the Third World. This, of course, is politically and strategically very different from the circumstances of the Falklands War.

All wars are unique, but it should be emphasised that the Falklands War was, in the second half of the twentieth century, an atypical and idiosyncratic instance of the long-range projection of military power. Lawrence Freedman commented: 'The limited and old-fashioned nature of the war should caution against trying to draw too much of wider significance out of the experience.'[26] The chances for a British defence of Hong Kong against the army of the People's Republic of China, just a few yards distant, if one imagines for a moment that such a defence is possible (it was not against the Japanese in 1942), are not enhanced by the Falklands experience; nor does the Falklands experience assist in any appreciable way the task of Western planners faced by, let us say, an incursion into Zaire by thousands of Soviet-supported Cuban troops or by a major Soviet military thrust towards the Gulf. The geo-strategic nature of the Falklands conflict was unique, and the British response will never be called upon to be repeated elsewhere because there are no similar commitments under similar threat. In the immediate aftermath of the fighting Field Marshal Lord Carver wrote: 'I can think of no other defence commitment for which the task force would have been suitable, not even the defence of Belize.'[27]

The conflict did provide a useful testing-ground for equipment and military tactics, but the strategic lessons to be drawn from it are very general, and in most instances hardly novel. None the less, if a British government ever considers a revival of a military role of consequence outside the NATO area, it should be done in full awareness of the strategic maxims which can be drawn from the Falklands episode. Britain could not project military force over such a distance without weakening its NATO defences and without calling upon considerable civilian support. The experience of the latter is to be welcomed and should act as an example and inspiration to military planners in the European theatre. The 1982 Defence White Paper, prepared before the invasion of the Falkland Islands, chose in a prescient manner to initiate a discussion of how best national resources could be used to assist the national defence effort.[28] The Falklands conflict has provided a most timely case-study. Over 110 ships were deployed, including 45 merchant ships whose civilian crews were all volunteers.[29] Overall, the logistics accomplishment was one of the outstanding features of the campaign.

However, the precedent of seriously weakening forces committed to NATO purposes to serve out-of-area commitments, even if it does illustrate the professionalism and flexibility of British forces, is not to be welcomed. The Ministry of Defence continues to stress that the major threat to British and NATO security post Falklands still emanates from Warsaw Pact forces in Europe, especially central Europe. In this regard the habit of depleting forces earmarked for NATO, which it is officially claimed are already overstretched, is not to be encouraged. The 5th Infantry Brigade, Britain's out-of-area 'strategic reserve', is to be further strengthened, in addition to the plans of the Defence Review of 1981, to enhance its capabilities to fulfil a military role outside the NATO area.[30] But for any contingency approaching Falklands proportions forces primarily committed to NATO duties would be required. If East–West tension had been high in Europe in April 1982 then it would have been most imprudent to have sent the task force. If a major crisis had developed between East and West in Europe in the spring and early summer of 1982, for example, in northern Europe (where British commando forces have a specific and vital role), then the British contribution to NATO would have been seriously impaired. If there is a definite policy to sustain a commitment, it is much better to have a credible deterrent *in situ* – and this lesson should not be lost on those advocating a weakening of BAOR – than to be forced to resort to arms following the failure of a diminished and neglected deterrent:

The deterrent value of forces on the spot is undeniable, and in retrospect it can be convincingly argued that the junta's refusal to believe that the British would fight for the Falklands was fatally encouraged by the absence of all but a token British force presence on the islands or in the South Atlantic prior to the Argentine invasion. It is highly doubtful whether the junta would have taken on a properly garrisoned Falklands supported by visibly robust British sea power in the area. Nor could Argentina have done so; the deterrent value of on-station forces is surpassed only by their war-fighting value.[31]

The role of naval power in the Falklands conflict has contributed to the considerable debate over the future shape and role of the Royal Navy, the eventual outcome of which will have important repercussions on the strategic direction of British defence policy. In the aftermath of the Falklands War the December 1982 Defence White Paper increased the projected size of RN surface front-line strength over the 1981 plans, and appeared to support the notion of a more balanced fleet.[32] However, these plans were more related to the extant South Atlantic commitment than constituting a victory for the naval lobby in the strategic debate.

Unquestionably the Falklands could not have been recovered without the major and vital contribution of the navy. The task force would never have reached the Falklands, and without carrier aviation and amphibious assault the islands would never have been retaken. In that regard, the balanced fleet and seaborne air power proved their worth. However, Britain has no other geo-strategic commitments similar to the Falkland Islands. Landing on a continental mainland, in Africa, the Middle East, or Europe, and engaging an indigenous or contiguous national army in strength is a very different exercise from surrounding a small group of islands 400 miles from the revisionist state and its air bases, and where internal lines of communication are so poor that seaborne amphibious forces can move faster and in greater force than the enemy on land.

But during the campaign, the Argentinian air force managed to sink six British ships, including two modern Type 42 air defence destroyers. Of the six vessels lost, only two were lost to surface-skimming missiles, while four were lost to old-fashioned 'gravity' bombs. At least six RN ships were hit by bombs which did not explode.[33] If a few had exploded then the task force would have suffered even more grievous naval losses, and might well have been obliged to return home.

Certainly the Royal Navy was not operating in an environment of its own choice, and there were equipment weaknesses, some of which will be remedied. Many vessels were obliged to spend time in confined waters such as Falkland Sound, and lacked early warning radar and sufficient air cover.[34] Yet the navy still shot down a lot of aircraft, and ship losses should not be unexpected in war anyway. However, when part of combined operations, supporting and supplying land forces, navies can rarely enjoy the luxury of choosing their battlefield. The Argentinian air force, not the most sophisticated of adversaries the Royal Navy could encounter in the foreseeable future, was not designed or trained for anti-shipping operations, many of its aircraft were over twenty years old, and it was operating at the extreme limit of its radius. Rio Gallegos, the nearest Argentinian air base, is 400 miles from the Falkland Islands. This allowed the Mirages and Skyhawks only a few minutes over their targets, and no time to fight back effectively against British aircraft. Once the Royal Navy had reached the Falklands the naval/air war raised severe questions about the vulnerability of surface vessels to land-based aircraft, especially if, in any future contingency, enemy land-based aircraft were nearer the fleet, had a specific anti-shipping role, were modern and were equipped with appropriate ordnance. An answer to such weakness is the provision of large-scale air support by traditional carrier task forces, but that is an expensive business:

> As Mr. Healey realised in 1966, unless one can provide naval air support on the scale which the large carriers of the US Navy provide (which, with the provision of escorts for them, is clearly beyond Britain's resources), naval surface operations, and especially those which tie the fleet to the land, are not possible against strong modern land-based air forces.[35]

The Falklands War did illustrate the utility of submarines in a variety of roles, and their effectiveness in fulfilling a number of duties at considerable distance from the home base with relative invulnerability:

> Our nuclear-powered submarines [SSNs] played a crucial role. After the sinking of the *General Belgrano* the Argentine surface fleet effectively took no further part in the campaign. The SSNs were flexible and powerful instruments throughout the crisis, posing a ubiquitous threat which the Argentines could neither measure nor oppose. Their spread and independence of support meant that they were the first assets to arrive in the South Atlantic, enabling us to declare a maritime exclusion zone early. They also provided valuable intelligence to our forces in the total exclusion zone.[36]

The decision of the Defence Review of 1981 to increase the number of the Royal Navy's nuclear hunter-killers from twelve to seventeen and to introduce a new class of diesel-powered submarines was sensible and realistic, and ought not to be allowed to slip. Submarines cannot transport task forces, but in terms of speed, deterrence, intelligence-gathering and strike power they are flexible, credible naval assets.

The importance of professional and trained military manpower was an old lesson re-emphasised by the British experience in the Falklands campaign. Despite the disparity in numbers, the British land forces were successful and the occupying Argentinian army was defeated. Both sides were well equipped – in some instances the Argentinians were better equipped – but the training (especially for cold weather and night fighting), organisation and leadership of the British forces yielded dividends. In the most testing climatic and topographical conditions the British commitment to long-serving volunteer forces, organised on the regimental basis, was vindicated.

In the short term the Falklands War was an outstanding British success. But in the longer term, what have been, or perhaps will be, the political and economic costs of recovering control of islands over which Britain had been negotiating for a number of years? The tentative conclusions reached are directly related to the Falklands episode, but they also throw some light on the kinds of cost, not always immediately obvious, that could be incurred by the long-range projection of military power elsewhere outside the NATO area. In an international system where states obey the rules and conventions of international behaviour only so long as they perceive it not to be in their vital interests not to break them, such a cost/gain calculation is apposite in assessing the decision to send the task force to the Falklands in the full knowledge that it ran a considerable risk of being drawn into hostilities.

As a foreign policy objective in its own right the retention of the Falkland Islands as a British colony is of dubious value. Port Stanley lacks the socio-economic infrastructure for either a major military base from which to police the South Atlantic if a significant threat was to emerge (some of the Argentinian ports are much more suited to that purpose), or a major base for the exploitation of oil or other mineral resources in that part of the South Atlantic if such a proposition becomes commercially or physically viable some day.

A major political cost to the West of British policy can be found in the deterioration of United States – Latin American relations. The shuttling of Secretary of State Haig in an attempt to negotiate a diplomatic solution illustrated the marked reluctance of the US government to take sides in the conflict, and it patently did not welcome being put in such a position. Latin America is a historic area of US influence, and is considered to be of immense geo-strategic importance. Since taking office the Reagan administration had been slowly and delicately attempting to construct a post-Carter Latin American strategy to counter what it perceives as a growing communist threat to United States hemispheric interests emanating from Central America. An important actor in this new strategy was to be Argentina, with the prospect of Argentinian forces being deployed in Central America in support of pro-Western governments. With the failure of diplomacy to solve the crisis, the United States was obliged to come down on the side of its major NATO ally. Although this decision was not taken until nearly a month after the invasion, considerable areas of Latin America have been alienated by United States policy. Hence, in an effort to salvage United States influence in many Latin American countries Washington has been trying to persuade London to reopen negotiations with Buenos Aires.

Another political cost of Britain's Falklands policy was to be found near to home. It appears that Britain's EEC partners did not welcome being obliged to impose economic sanctions on Argentina, as witnessed by their insistence, in the first instance, on imposing sanctions for no more than two weeks rather than making the more open-ended commitment which the British government would have preferred.[37] When the initial period of sanctions came to an end there was considerable prevarication over their extension, especially by Ireland, with a long tradition of hostility to British colonialism, and by Italy, with a large expatriate population in Argentina. Furthermore, the replacement of Lord Carrington as Foreign Secretary by Francis Pym, inexperienced in EEC affairs and absorbed by the Falklands dispute, led to a neglect and mishandling of some intra-EEC business.

Longer-term political costs of the British policy could be a considerable reduction in British influence in Latin America, and perhaps the emergence of a much more nationalistic, less pro-Western, non-aligned government in Buenos Aires, which could begin to influence neighbouring states historically susceptible to the tone and direction of Argentinian politics.

Over and above any commercial business lost to Britain because of its Falklands policy, the major direct economic costs are to be found in the cost of the task force, the material losses suffered by the task force and the cost of garrisoning the islands. The task force operation, from April to September 1982, cost £700m., which was met from the government's reserve contingency fund of £2,500m. Replacement of material lost in the campaign over the three years 1982–5 will total about £900m.[38] The material replacement costs will be borne by the Treasury. Garrisoning the islands with 3,000–4,000 men, providing air support and defence and having two or three warships and a submarine on patrol could cost only a few million pounds if provided from current forces. But this would stretch further the already severely stretched forces committed to NATO, and also reduce the flexibility of British forces in the event of any other crisis outside the NATO area where a British presence is deemed essential. The December 1982 Defence White Paper announced that the monies required to maintain a substantial garrison in the Falkland Islands would be found from resources additional to the antebellum defence budget and its projected annual 3 per cent increase in real terms until 1985/6.[39] However, it is questionable for how long the Falklands garrison costs can be perceived and politically accepted as 'something apart' from the defence budget. Expenditure of £300m.–£400m. on the South Atlantic commitment will reduce the room for manoeuvre of the mainstream defence budget when, by the mid-1980s, re-equipment programmes will be stretching resources committed to Britain's NATO and independent nuclear deterrent objectives. It is to be feared that the open-ended Falklands commitment could put into jeopardy the level and quality of Britain's conventional contribution to NATO.

It could be argued that on any rational appraisal the loss of 250 British lives, expenditure of over £1·5 billion (cost of operation plus loss of material), other costs such as £35m. for lengthening Stanley airfield, and the long-term political and diplomatic costs, were disproportionate to the gains of the policy.

A retort could be that politics is not logic, that the Falklands policy incorporated the sustenance of deeply held values, of moral imperatives and the rule that dictators should not be appeased. In reply one could adopt the Weberian perspective that the real morality of any action is to be found more in its consequence than in the action itself. Without doubt, the 'worth' of the Falklands War of 1982 is a matter of personal judgement, but there should be an awareness of the results and the costs of the decision to project and to use military force.

All conflicts are unique, but the Falklands War was exceptional. Satisfaction may be derived from the logistical achievements of the campaign, the marrying of civilian and military resources and the evident quality of British servicemen in hostile conditions. But to suggest that the Falklands experience supports arguments for an expanded surface fleet and a return to a major power-projection role beyond the North Atlantic is seriously to misunderstand some of the strategic lessons of the conflict and to underestimate the political and economic costs. It is most unlikely that the next extra-North Atlantic conflict into which the British could be tempted if the means were to hand would be in defence of a tiny British colony, isolated from a vast hinterland by over 400 miles of ocean, against the well-equipped but poorly trained and commanded forces of a shaky South American dictatorship.

Notes: Chapter 6

1   *Statement on Defence Estimates 1970*, Cmnd 4290 (London: HMSO, 1970), ch. 1, p. 6, para. 28.
2   See *Statement on Defence Estimates 1975*, Cmnd 5976 (London: HMSO, 1975).
3   'The British Defence Review', *The World Today*, vol. 31, no. 4 (1975), p. 132.
4   See Lawrence Freedman, 'Britain's contribution to NATO', *International Affairs*, vol. 56, no. 1 (1978), p. 36.
5   For a discussion of the role of BAOR in European security see John Garnett, 'BAOR and NATO', *International Affairs*, vol. 46, no. 4 (1970), pp. 670–81.
6   See *The United Kingdom Defence Programme: The Way Forward*, Cmnd 8288 (London: HMSO, 1981), pp. 9–10, paras 21–31.
7   See 'Unnoticed anniversary marks army's eight years in Ulster', *The Times*, 15 August 1977, p. 2; and J. Brian Garett, 'Ten years of British troops in Northern Ireland', *International Security*, vol. 4, no. 3 (1979/80), pp. 80–92.
8   For an illustration of the arguments see David Greenwood, *The Polaris Successor System: At What Cost?*, ASIDE No. 16 (Aberdeen: Centre for Defence Studies, 1980), and 'Strategic virtue, economic necessity', *Defence Attaché*, no. 6 (1980), pp. 15–20.
9   See Tony Geraghty, 'Retreat to Fortress Britain', *Sunday Times*, 4 January 1981, p. 17.
10 See David Fairhall, 'Now, a political fight for the surface ship', *Guardian*, 18 June 1982, p. 2.
11 See Harold Wilson, *The Labour Government 1964–1970. A Personal Record* (London: Weidenfeld & Nicolson, 1970), pp. 625–6.
12 See *Report on World Affairs* (London), April–June 1980, pp. 37–8, and July–September 1980, pp. 42–3; and 'Pacific mesentente', *The Economist*, 21 June 1980, p. 14.
13 See 'Belize: waiting for its enemies to fall', *Guardian*, 15 February 1980, p. 7.
14 See 'Cays and effect', *The Economist*, 21 March 1981, pp. 71–2.

15   See 'Belize freedom brings attack on UK', *Guardian*, 27 July 1982, p. 1; 'Threatened Belize want UK troops to stay on', *Observer*, 20 September 1981, p. 7; and *The Economist*, 12 September 1981, p. 48, and 26 September 1981, p. 58.

16   See R. P. Owen, 'The rebellion in Dhofar – a threat to Western interests in the Gulf', *The World Today*, vol. 29, no. 6 (1973), pp. 266–72.

17   See contributions by Henry Stanhope and Tim Owen to the 'Oman' supplement, *The Times*, 18 November 1976, p. vi, and Mark Malloch Brown, 'Oman: a report', *The Economist*, 11 August 1979, pp. 57–68.

18   See Bard O'Neill, 'Revolutionary war in Oman', in Bard O'Neill *et al.* (eds), *Insurgency in the Modern World* (Boulder, Colo: Westview Press, 1980), p. 225.

19   See Robert Fisk, 'Young Britons hold the line in Oman', *The Times*, 30 April 1981, p. 10.

20   See Martin Woolacott, 'Oman leader presses Thatcher for support', *Guardian*, 24 April 1981, p. 6.

21   See Peter Calvocoressi, *World Politics Since 1945* (London: Longman, 1970), p. 125.

22   J. D. B. Miller, *Survey of Commonwealth Affairs: Problems of Expansion and Attrition 1953–1969* (London: Oxford University Press, 1974), p. 374.

23   For details of the disposition of British non-NATO forces, see *Statement on the Defence Estimates 1982*, Cmnd 8529–1 (London: HMSO, 1982), pp. 14–15.

24   See Sunday Times Insight Team, *The Falklands War* (London: Sphere, 1982), ch. 19, pp. 209–16.

25   See 'Too much on the Rhine', *The Times*, 1 July 1982, p. 13.

26   Lawrence Freedman, 'The War of the Falkland Islands, 1982', *Foreign Affairs*, vol. 61, no. 1 (1982), p. 196.

27   Field Marshal Lord Carver, letter to *The Times*, 23 June 1982, p. 11.

28   See 'Use of national resources', *Statement on the Defence Estimates 1982*, op. cit., pp. 17–18.

29   See *The Falklands Campaign: The Lessons*, Cmnd 8758 (London: HMSO, 1982), p. 6, para. 106.

30   ibid., p. 32, para. 304.

31   Jeffrey Record, 'The Falklands War', *Washington Quarterly*, vol. 5, no. 4 (1982), p. 48.

32   See *The Falklands Campaign: The Lessons*, op. cit., pp. 33–4, paras 307–11.

33   See Robert Chesshyre, 'Dud bombs "cost junta war" ', *Observer*, 1 August 1982, p. 1.

34   See Freedman, 'The War of the Falkland Islands, 1982', op. cit., p. 208.

35   Lord Carver, op. cit.

36   See *The Falklands Campaign: The Lessons*, op. cit., p. 17, para. 211.

37   See John Palmer, 'Just how far will Europe back Mrs Thatcher', *Guardian*, 15 April 1982, p. 13.

38   Rodney Cowton, 'Falkland war costs top £1,600m', *The Times*, 29 October 1982, p. 1.

39   See *The Falklands Campaign: The Lessons*, op. cit., pp. 32–3, para. 306.

7 Prescription

The French interventions in Zaire in 1977 and 1978, and elsewhere in Africa in the late 1970s,[1] illustrate the type of intervention which may be open to European medium-rank powers: short and sharp, in areas of traditional influence, involving only very limited forces, and for generally perceived admirable motives such as political stabilisation or the protection of human life. Giscard d'Estaing always argued that French interventions were of such a character, in sharp contrast to the classic 'colonial' strategy pursued by the Soviet-supported Cuban forces in Angola (20,000 Cuban troops) and Ethiopia (17,000 Cuban troops) where large forces have been deployed over the past few years and continue to be. In the recent civil war in Chad, the most enduring and major French military involvement in Africa, no more than 1,800 French troops (including a large number of advisers) were ever present.

Nevertheless, even such limited interventions as the French have recently conducted in Africa, when most of the prerequisites for successful intervention were in evidence – legitimacy, realisable political objectives and public support – considerable operational and logistical problems have been encountered. In Zaire in 1977 the Shaba intervention was complicated by the paucity of French long-range air-lift capability, and assistance was provided by the Moroccan air force. In the 1978 Shaba intervention logistical problems were even worse.[2] Private jet aircraft had to be requisitioned and a plea made to the United States for low-key military assistance in the form of air-lift to transport the French Foreign Legionnaires to Zaire.[3] The Foreign Legion also had to borrow parachutes from the Zaire army, which resulted in more casualties than did the hostilities once on the ground. As a direct result of such experiences plans were being implemented to increase French long-range air-lift capability, and a special unit of three regiments of paratroops was being trained for long-range intervention in Africa and the Middle East. Manoeuvres have taken place in Zaire since 1978. However, such plans are now in doubt as President Mitterrand has pledged to reverse the Giscardian policy of intervention, though France will honour present defence commitments to francophone states in Africa.[4]

Certainly, given the resources and the will, an intervention and stability-inducing role for a European medium-rank power is not out of the question. In the British instance, paying heed to the lessons of Suez and with a combination of political will, barely adequate capabilities and the appropriate political context, Britain undertook a successful decade of interventions following the Suez crisis of 1956. However, is the intervention environment in the 1980s similarly conducive to the long-range projection of military power? One suspects that the prevailing mood in Reagan-Republican America would applaud and support such endeavours, but severe question marks would exist over British and European perceptions. A vital element in any intervention would be the level not only of public support but, especially in Britain, of bipartisan political support. Such support did exist for British ventures of a limited nature in the 1956–66 decade, but the current radical defence trends in the British Labour Party and the growing mood of pacifism in some vocal sections of the British and West European public appear to rule out the expectation of automatic support for, or indifference towards, the use of military force outside the NATO area.

Another major problem is that of capabilities. The 1956–66 decade for Britain, and the French experiences in Africa, though successful, did reveal the kinds of capability and resource problems medium-rank powers encounter when undertaking long-distance military interventions. Considerable risks were taken when resources were stretched to the limit. With the rundown of British interventionary capabilities over the past fifteen years, independent military intervention overseas is out of the question unless a government is prepared to take enormous risks. Even if the conflict does not involve the forces or proxy-forces of advanced military powers, the acquisition by less developed states of cheap, easily operated, sophisticated modern weapons of great accuracy and fire-power – in addition to the operational and logistical problems encountered in deploying military force far from home – requires that considerable caution be exercised. This is especially so if the incursion of a Western developed state could lead to a direct clash with Soviet military forces.[5]

Independent British military action was deemed imprudent in Rhodesia in 1965–6, and even in the European theatre in 1974. Although the will may be returning in some quarters of British public life, the resources to sustain a British rapid deployment force capable of sustained independent action, probably in extreme heat, and with severely stretched and limited lines of supply and communication, are not available, and are even less likely to be made available in the foreseeable future if the current emphasis of British defence resists any deflection by the Falklands experience.[6] The Conservative government appears to have faced up to this resource problem. Mr John Nott, when Secretary of State for Defence, spoke in the House of Commons on 17 March 1981 of a 'modest use of force to protect the interests of friendly local states and of the West in strategic regions'. This followed a television interview on 8 March when the Defence Secretary spoke of a 'company-sized intervention, or at the most a battalion'.[7] The 1981 Defence White Paper confirmed these images of a very limited intervention capability. Mention was made of a 'special equipment stockpile for limited operations overseas', of 'stretching' the RAF's thirty Hercules aircraft to increase capacity over short ranges by the equivalent of eight new aircraft, of a limited parachute assault capability trained to drop an entire battalion in fifteen minutes, of improvement of command and control for overseas operations, and of a headquarters and staff earmarked for such operations.[8] With such limited forces it is obviously expected that any traditional intervention will be conducted in conjunction with allies. Other West European states and, naturally, the United States are the likely partners.

In the first instance, collaboration with West European states which are also EEC partners or fellow members of NATO's Eurogroup is appealing. However, upon further examination three major problems are encountered. First, there is no institutional mechanism equipped for the task. NATO includes non-West European and non-EEC powers, and has geographical limits to its jurisdiction. Even if NATO could be committed to military action south of the Tropic of Cancer such a decision would require approval of the NATO Council, and there is no guarantee that the North American perception of the crisis would coincide with the European, nor that they would agree over appropriate responses. Indeed, it is highly unlikely that all the Eurogroup countries would be in close agreement about appropriate policy over a faraway crisis. Any attempt to use NATO or subgroups within NATO for such purposes could be most detrimental to the overall health of the Alliance. The EEC is not, primarily, a foreign and defence policy making body. It is only now, in the 1980s, that the EEC is painfully and tortuously attempting to create and implement a very few foreign policies over which all its members can agree. For the foreseeable future it appears likely that the EEC's strategic role will continue to be played via its economic policies towards the developing countries.

The second major obstacle to West European collaboration over long-distance military intervention is public opinion. Elements of public opinion in Britain and France may support extra-European military roles reminiscent of former imperial glories but it is most unlikely that public opinion in West Germany, the Netherlands, Belgium, Denmark and the Irish Republic would cheer such enterprises, for a variety of socio-economic, political and ethical reasons.[9]

The third major problem is that of capabilities. Even assuming agreement over foreign policy objectives and strategy, and the requisite public support, do the major West European states possess the required military capabilities?[10] Logistic support is the major weakness but, for a very short and limited operation, Anglo-French-Belgian forces composed of air-portable marines and parachute battalions[11] could fulfil a number of tasks, assuming smooth command and control and cohesive inter-operability. The Federal Republic of Germany has the largest army in West Europe, which includes three air-transportable brigades, but historical and constitutional factors inhibit the deployment of West German forces outside the European theatre. However, to date, the Franco-Belgian example in Shaba and the Anglo-French example in the New Hebrides do not stand out as shining illustrations of how well West European sovereign states can work together in the management of common extra-European problems.

The most likely and inevitably the most senior partner of any collaborative intervention in which British forces may participate in the near future would be the United States. Mrs Thatcher has publicly supported the concept of the United States Rapid Deployment Force, and has encouraged notions of British military support in the implementation of the Carter Doctrine if required. Proclaimed in January 1980 in immediate response to the Soviet invasion of Afghanistan, and against the backdrop of a perceived major Soviet threat in the less developed world, especially the Gulf region, the Carter Doctrine has not been disowned by the Reagan administration. On the contrary, the Carter Doctrine forms the doctrinal basis for the Reagan administration's support for the RDF concept, and the massive planned build-up of United States conventional forces. In January 1980 President Carter declared:

> Let our position be absolutely clear: an attempt by any outside force to gain control of the Persian Gulf region will be regarded as an assault on the vital interests of the United States of America and such an assault will be repelled by any means necessary, including military force.

The foreign policy ethos and will developed in the later stages of the Carter administration have taken root and flowered in the Reagan administration. The Gulf remains the focus of attention in Washington, but further Soviet threats to vital Western interests elsewhere in the developing world are coming to fall under the doctrinal aegis inherited from the previous administration.

However, even in the company of a superpower which welcomes British support, primarily for domestic and international political reasons, a number of potential problems present themselves. Is it correct always to assume a coinciding perception and interpretation of any threat? Given the American proclivity to identify a 'communist' threat and a Soviet 'military' threat [12] as one and the same, and the tendency of the West Europeans (though admittedly the continental West Europeans more than the British) to draw some distinction between the two, disagreements over threat assessment and the appropriate reaction to certain sorts of disturbance in strategically important regions are not beyond possibility. In this context a related problem for the British is that the British contribution to any Anglo-American RDF is bound to constitute very much the minor part. In an Anglo-American force of over 100,000 men, the British contingent could well number less than 1,000, plus a small naval contribution. In such circumstances command and control would inevitably be in United States political and military hands. The prospect of command and control disagreement is heightened by the current confusion over the exact role of the RDF. Does Washington see the RDF as a conventional deterrent to Soviet attack, or a 'trip-wire' to signal nuclear readiness, or a tool to control *coups d'état* and local civil wars, or a force to rescue friendly local regimes, or perhaps an occupation army to secure the sources of vital raw materials (maybe against the wishes of the local regime)?

In the event of disagreement, whether over grand strategy (e.g. is it possible to engage Soviet forces in the Gulf region without being at war in central Europe?) or battlefield tactics (e.g. does one introduce tactical nuclear weapons into the conflict?), what does the minor partner do? Do the British, perhaps much against their better political or military judgement, blindly follow the United States into the fray, or are political and military support withheld as the United States 'goes it alone', and Anglo-American and maybe North Atlantic Alliance relations are severely damaged?

On paper the United States RDF is impressive. It can call upon the army's 82nd Airborne Division, the 101st Airborne Division (Air Assault), and 24th Mechanised Infantry Division, and the 9th Infantry Division, plus Ranger and Special Forces Units. The Marine Corps could contribute a Marine Amphibious force of a division and an air wing, and the 7th Marine Amphibious Brigade. The RDF's air power includes tactical fighter wings of F15s and F111s, reconnaissance squadrons and tactical air-lift squadrons. There would be at least one naval combat task force operating with the RDF. However, even with pre-positioned (in the right place?) merchant ships containing supplies, logistics is a major problem for the United States. In the Gulf area a combat-ready battalion could be on the ground within forty-eight hours, but it would be a week before a brigade-size group followed, a fortnight before an airborne division could be in place, and a month before an additional division would have arrived by sea. For a force of only 80,000 operating in the Gulf region fuel and water supplies alone would demand a lift capacity of 9,600 tons per day.[13] By air from the United States to the Gulf is 7,000 miles, and by sea 12,000 miles. Sea transport is much slower, but a single C-4 cargo ship can carry the ammunition equivalent of 500 sorties by a C-141 aircraft. Hence there has been pressure from the Pentagon for a large permanent base in the Gulf area, as well as the conclusion of agreements with Somalia, Kenya and Oman for the upgrading of base facilities to United States military standards, and the use of these facilities in the event of hostilities.

However, in view of the expense and complexity of RDF planning, how real and immediate is the Soviet military threat to the Gulf region? Does it demand such massive contingency forces? In any threat to the Gulf, which would be such a direct threat to vital Western interest that it is probable only in the context of a major East–West conflict, the Soviets would encounter severe logistical and tactical problems over the extremely hostile and mountainous terrain between the southern USSR and the Gulf, or between Afghanistan and the Gulf. Soviet forces obliged to cross the mountain passes of the region could find progress severely hindered by indigenous forces, or small-scale United States forces, or low-level tactical nuclear attack, and would be most vulnerable to air attack.[14] In such a scenario even a small United States force would be useful as a signal of resolve and a potential tripwire prior to escalation. The Soviet army concentrates on shock and short war tactics, and organises its forces accordingly. It is generally accepted that

Soviet divisions lack staying power and sustainability. The 'tail' of the Soviet army is relatively short, and as a result logistic support units are kept to a minimum. Hence 'Soviet ability to sustain its ground forces in conflict for long periods of time or over great distances has always been somewhat suspect.'[15]

Airborne military transport capabilities in supplying Soviet-proxy forces in Ethiopia and Angola have been impressive, but always unopposed by sophisticated hostile air forces, or any air force at all. Soviet frontal aviation is impressive in sheer size, with more than 5,000 fixed-wing combat aircraft, but the whole force is trained and structured to fight a European war as an extension of Soviet artillery. About three-quarters of Soviet front-line combat air capability is in Eastern Europe or the western military districts of the Soviet Union. With no forward-based air controllers (unlike the United States forces) flexibility is very limited, and a low premium is attached to pilot initiative. As Soviet frontal aviation also has poor in-flight refuel capabilities, all these factors make it difficult for Moscow to deploy its combat air power over long distances. The Soviet navy has undergone dramatic growth in the past twenty years, creating considerable concern in the West, and much debate over the purpose of the Soviet naval build-up: is it to show the flag, or is it primarily to project military power, or is the development of the navy the result of internal institutional rivalry?[16] However, it is important to note that Soviet naval infantry is small in contrast to the United States Marine Corps. Soviet naval infantry numbers only 12,000 in five regiments, spread around all the fleets. Unlike the United States Marines it has little staying power, and can operate independently for only four or five days at the most. The primary role of the Soviet naval infantry is probably on the European flanks in a major European war; for example, seizing and holding the Dardanelles until land or air support arrives. The Soviet navy's ability to fight a long sea war is hampered by its poor replenishment and rearming-at-sea capabilities both in terms of numbers (the US ratio is 1:15 while the Soviet ratio is 1:42) and in technique; for instance, the Soviet replenishment-at-sea is considerably slower than the United States method. Furthermore, geography presents a serious obstacle to the projection of sea-based or naval-supported Soviet military power if faced by Western navies, as the four Soviet fleets are widely separated – the Northern Fleet, the Baltic Fleet, the Black Sea Fleet and the Pacific Ocean Fleet – and outside the Warsaw Pact area have very few ports and anchorages secure in themselves, or with secure hinterlands. One commentator puts the Soviet long-range military threat into the following perspective:

> Restrictions upon Soviet force projection capabilities should not be interpreted to mean that the USSR is impotent. It is not. In fact, the Kremlin leaders have developed a formidable military structure . . . Soviet military capabilities and improved equipment obviously present the USSR with opportunities heretofore not available. The Soviet Union is now involved in areas of the

world where it traditionally had never ventured ... However to keep the Soviet challenge in proper perspective it is necessary to look at more than quantities of equipment. It is important to recognise that the Soviet Union's force structure also can restrict Soviet military capabilities and options available to Kremlin decisionmakers ... Even after taking the Afghanistan invasion into consideration, Soviet military capabilities for the 1980s will primarily remain at the influence end of the force projection continuum ... The recent invasion of Afghanistan occurred within that arc of primary Soviet geo-political advantage ... These conditions of Soviet advantage which maximised Soviet military capabilities in Afghanistan may not exist as one moves further from Soviet borders.[17]

A more proportionate and cost-effective way to enhance the security of far-away places of vital strategic importance than the provision of large-scale, high profile Western intervention forces would be the encouragement of purely regional pacts of like-minded pro-Western states. Certainly, residual forces earmarked for intervention operations could be called upon *in extremis*, as a signal of resolve, or commitment, or as a trip-wire, but such scenarios could be made less likely by the construction of regional pacts. Again, in this regard the Gulf is a focus of attention, and Britain has given considerable encouragement to the notion of a Gulf Pact. In March 1981 six Gulf states, Saudi Arabia, Kuwait, Bahrain, Qatar, the United Arab Emirates and Oman announced their intention to form the Gulf Co-operation Council (GCC). Rather than military alliance or a political federation, it is planned that the GCC will work for economic harmonisation and very gradual political co-operation. The GCC is not a defence pact, but concern over security, especially internal security, in the light of the fall of the Shah, the occupation of the Grand Mosque in Mecca, the Soviet invasion of Afghanistan and the Iran–Iraq War, is what has brought the states together. There is nearly unanimous agreement that the major security threat is not from a Soviet military thrust into the area, though there is the recognition that this is not entirely improbable. Except for Oman, all the GCC members have stated that Western protection 'on the ground' is not required or welcome as it would increase rather than diminish the risk of Soviet intervention. Opponents of suggestions that fully fledged Western bases should be situated in the Gulf region argue that clumping Western soldiery would merely exacerbate the internal political and religious problems of the rapidly modernising but anciently administered states of the Gulf region, especially as most have large, volatile expatriate populations. Saudi Arabia has been most vocal in opposing the United States suggestion for a full-blown military base on Saudi soil, arguing that such a direct military presence could well draw the Soviets into the region's affairs through increased support for internal subversion.[18]

A two-day inaugural summit of heads of state in May 1981 saw the GCC launched, with Abdullah Bishara, former Kuwaiti Ambassador to the United Nations, as its first secretary-general. Undoubtedly the GCC will experience strong differences of opinion on many matters among its members but its existence does display a readiness, at least, to put aside some traditional rivalries in the search for security:

> The aim is to reduce the possibility of regional instability affecting Gulf populations or spreading from one Gulf state to another. Improved co-ordination of economic and social development and internal security matters will help contain tensions. There is a recognised need for industrial consultations to limit wasteful duplication, the growth of immigrant work forces and un-settling inter-Emirate competition.[19]

Whatever the realities of the Soviet military threat to strategically important areas contiguous to the Soviet Union may be (the geo-strategic thrust and direction of Soviet military capabilities could change, but hardly in a major way in the short term), and whatever the requirements are for internal stability in such regions, there is a genuine perception in many public and private bodies in the West that there is a real and immediate Soviet military threat to areas of vital economic and strategic interest to the developed democracies. In response to such perceived threats 1981 witnessed the publication, *inter alia*, of two reports recommending not merely the improvement of Western military capabilities to counter the Soviet military threat, but the development of new international associations of the major Western industrial powers,[20] or regional alliances sponsored by and including the major Western powers, and also perhaps Japan,[21] able to introduce strong military forces into the threatened areas. In both reports it is envisaged that Britain should play a substantial role in the provision of naval and land forces, and in one of the reports even propaganda forces,[22] to counter the extra-North Atlantic threat.

However, not only would such international arrangements antagonise the smaller NATO, EEC and other interested powers excluded from decision-making which may affect their security, and not only do such plans run contrary to the clearly expressed wishes of most developing countries not to have Western forces visibly in the region and to be seen to be responsible for their own security, but the fundamental political prerequisites for successful multilateral security pacts would, in all likelihood, be in short supply or even absent.

Military alliances in the contemporary world of competitive states are single-purpose entities sustained by a basic underlying community of interest which is recognised by all the members to be of greater importance than all the lesser issues which may divide them. It is the single-nature purpose of alliances which distinguishes them from multi-purpose, multilateral organisations, such as the EEC, where no single concern is predominant and bargaining over a whole range of issues may take place. Unlike the Atlantic Alliance, the perception of a common enemy or the contemplation of military engagement and war plays an insignificant role, if any role at all. The pre-eminent foreign policy objective of all states is to guarantee the security of the state, and security is the single purpose around which alliances are invariably built. A common threat is perceived and a number of states decide to aggregate their power to face the common threat. But security in the face of the common threat must retain its high priority in the hierarchy of foreign policy interests of the participating states. Otherwise, if other state interests, such as economic competition with allies, or the development of unequal perceptions of the threat undermines the common security bond, the alliance will crumble. The common denominator will have disappeared. Is it likely that such geographically distant and economically competitive states such as Britain, Japan, the United States, the Federal Republic of Germany, Canada and France could sustain a unanimous and consistently high perception of the threat to vital interests in faraway places? Could the publics of these states be convinced? The whole question becomes even more problematical if one includes regional powers such as Saudi Arabia, Zaire, or the Republic of South Africa in the apposite security pacts.

In this regard, the lesson of the North Atlantic Alliance, a most successful multilateral security pact, must be that if interests and membership are sufficiently limited then an alliance will endure for a long time.[23] Any expansion of the *casus foederis* of an alliance, especially in peacetime, increases the likelihood of internal conflict which in turn contributes towards destabilisation of the international system: 'precise definitions of scope, *casus foederis*, and obligations lend predictability to the responses alliance partners will make in crisis situations. Predictability is an important element in international stability and may become crucial in crisis situations.'[24]

The implementation of suggestions to construct new security pacts outside NATO would merely institutionalise expectations which could not always be delivered. Indeed, the more sensitive the crisis the more likely that allies far-distant from the scene would disagree, but international opinion (including the Soviet Union) would be looking for coherent, cohesive responses, and in their absence perhaps act accordingly. Such inflexible diplomatic and defence arrangements would be inimical to Western security.

Such are the political and military complexities of projecting military power over considerable distances to achieve foreign policy objectives, *vis-à-vis* allies as well as adversaries, that Britain (and other interested West European medium-rank powers) ought to desist from the temptation to seek out an interventionary role in the developing world's trouble spots. If it is thought desirable to have a military capability available to act as a trip-wire, or a deterrent, or a defensive force, then the United States should be encouraged to act unilaterally. For the West, this would constitute the most politically and operationally cost-effective organisation of intervention. While the United States could agree broad strategic policy with the West European allies, tactical control and direction would remain in United States hands. If some physical manifestation of West European strategic and diplomatic support is deemed necessary then a limited 'over the horizon' naval contribution would operationally and politically be the most cost-effective. West European (including British) forces perform a much more important function in Europe, and greater 'value-for-money' is derived from large West

European forces on the Central Front, enhancing deterrence and raising the nuclear threshold, and thereby allowing more flexibility for United States forces:

> The idea – much discussed during the year – of European contingents assisting the American military presence in the Gulf region has its merits, less in the sense of military efficiency than in demonstrating to the Soviet Union and reassuring the United States that she was not alone. But to dilute West European military efforts in order to become involved, if only symbolically, in meeting the new security threat outside Europe would risk making them marginally relevant there and inadequate at home where their primary task will continue to lie.[25]

It appears to be a hard fact of the reality of the international system that, in the late twentieth century, Britain and other West European powers are vulnerable to adverse events in strategically important but faraway places around the globe. Events in the Gulf and Central Africa are essentially outside the close control of West European powers unless politically sensitive decisions are taken to devote massive resources, in a collaborative manner, to equip, maintain, base and organise military interventionary forces, about whose use the involved parties could then agree over the long term. Even then, as the United States discovered in South-East Asia in the 1960s when exercising massive military force, success requires a reasonable level of indigenous political support in the target region, and quiescent public opinion at home. At least in the 1960s a risk-wary Soviet Union cautiously remained on the sidelines of many Third World conflicts. There is less reason to assume this will always be the case in the 1980s and 1990s.

It could be argued that the actions most conducive to security in the long term are those essentially domestic policies which reduce excessive dependence on imported raw materials, especially oil, from vulnerable areas of the less developed world. For example, is it not time that the provision of clean, cheap and convenient public transport systems in the advanced industrial societies came to be appreciated and generally understood as a strategic asset with immense foreign policy implications? Similarly, government subsidies for, and encouragement of, the coal industry in the West should be viewed in this light. Britain and the United States are particularly fortunate in this regard, as both have several hundred years' worth of accessible coal reserves. One suspects that governments, especially in West Europe, could 'sell' cheaper government-supported public transport fares and coal subsidies to the electorate as legitimate Exchequer expenditure much more easily than expensive, risk-taking military intervention forces.

Furthermore, a change of regime contrary to the wishes of Western governments does not automatically mean a political loss to the West or the discontinuation of trade. Recent evidence suggests that, regardless of the declaratory ideological complexions and allegiances of new governments in the developing world, many such governments seek out, later if not sooner, the best customers and trading partners available. In the case of Angola, very soon after the victory of the Marxist forces in the civil war Gulf Oil was invited to develop the oil resources of the state. Prime Minister Mugabe of Zimbabwe has made his preference for doing business with the West rather than the East abundantly clear. President Machel of Mozambique has publicly repented his reluctance to maintain trade links with the West, and is actively seeking greater commercial contact with the capitalist world.

Nevertheless, it is indisputable that there is considerable political instability in the developing world. Conflict within states and between states appears endemic, and in many instances strategic and economic interests of the West can be at high risk, regardless of efforts to minimise vulnerabilities. Regimes friendly towards the liberal democratic world may be under threat or attack, and continued access to important raw materials put in jeopardy. Circumstances could arise where military force might appear as an attractive policy option but, for a medium-rank power such as Britain, only specific types of commitments ought to be considered. British operations in Oman in the 1970s and the Franco-Belgian interventions in Zaire in 1977 and 1978 are the best illustrations of the sort of military interventions which can be contemplated. In Oman British forces, in a low-key manner, were assisting the indigenous army of a pro-Western administration. The commitment was by invitation, it was limited, it was composed of a few highly skilled personnel and it was in support of an established ruler with a strong domestic base. The second instance was of an invited, short, sharp military intervention, unavoidably public, but in pursuit of a clear and laudable objective, namely, the protection of human life. Great care was taken to withdraw the forces very soon after the operation.

Apart from such closely restricted scenarios it is imprudent for Britain to use military forces in support of foreign policy objectives in faraway places. If the crisis is of a larger nature than those described above, and the commitment demanded greater, then the prospect of escalation is increased and the capacity of British resources to match the task less likely. As discussed above, if a major crisis arises in the developing world which threatens vital Western interests and requires a potentially large and costly military input then, for reasons of cohesive command and control and sound intra-Alliance relations, the United States should be encouraged to shoulder the burden. If, for whatever reason, Britain undertakes a limited interventionary commitment alone, or in symbolic support of a major United States effort, the circumstances must be right. The lessons of the Suez intervention and the experience of the subsequent decades must be paid due heed. The action should have sound moral foundations; the legal basis for the intervention must be clear; military capabilities need to be adequate for the task to hand; policy consensus with the United States is vital; and the political purpose of the use of military force must be unambiguous.

Notes: Chapter 7

1 See Pierre Lellouche and Dominique Moisi, 'French policy in Africa: a lonely battle against destabilisation', *International Security*, vol. 3, no. 4 (1979), pp. 121–3.
2 See Paul Webster, 'France to drop troops in Zaire as warning to rebels', *Guardian*, 11 September 1979, p. 7.
3 See Alex Gliksman, 'Three keys for Europe's bombs', *Foreign Policy*, no. 39 (1980), p. 48.
4 See Colin Legum, 'Man of principle takes over at Quai d'Orsay', *Observer*, 24 May 1981, p. 8.
5 See R. Osgood, 'The post-war strategy of limited war: before, during and after Vietnam', in Laurence Martin (ed.), *Strategic Thought in the Nuclear Age* (London: Heinemann, 1979), p. 128.
6 See David Fairhall, 'Rapid but not cheap', *Guardian*, 3 March 1981, p. 15; Tony Geraghty, 'Slow take-off for Mrs. T's rapid force', *Sunday Times*, 8 March 1981, p. 14; and Keith Hartley, 'Can the UK afford a rapid deployment force', *RUSIJ*, vol. 127, no. 1 (1982), pp. 18–22.
7 See *Defence Attaché*, no. 2 (1981), p. 5.
8 See *Statement on Defence Estimates 1981*, Cmnd. 8212–1 (London: HMSO, 1981), p. 32, para. 416.
9 See François Duchêne, 'The strategic consequences of the enlarged European Community', *Survival*, vol. XV, no. 1 (1973), p. 6.
10 For an assessment of the West European forces which could be made available for deployment in the extra-North Atlantic area see P. Foot, *Beyond the North Atlantic: The European Contribution*, ASIDE No. 21 (Aberdeen: Centre for Defence Studies, 1982).
11 See Air Marshal Sir Frederick Sowrey, 'Western military capabilities in the Middle East', *NATO's Fifteen Nations*, vol. 25, no. 5 (1980), p. 32.
12 See David W. Tarr, 'Political constraints on United States intervention in low-intensity conflicts', *Parameters. Journal of the US Army War College*, vol. X, no. 3 (1980), pp. 56–7.
13 See *Strategic Survey 1980–81* (London: IISS, 1981), p. 5.
14 See Robert Harvy, 'Defending the Gulf: a survey', *The Economist*, 6 June 1981, p. 34.
15 Keith A. Dunn, 'Power projection or influence: Soviet capabilities for the 1980s', *Naval War College Review*, 1980, p. 34.
16 For an insight into the arguments see Bradford Dismukes and James McConnell (eds), *Soviet Naval Diplomacy* (Oxford: Pergamon, 1979); and Michael MccGwire (ed.), *Soviet Naval Developments* (London: Praeger, 1973).
17 Dunn, op. cit., pp. 46–7.
18 See Robert Stephens, 'Saudis tell US to think again', *Observer*, 12 April 1981, p. 10.
19 Valerie Yorke, *Guardian*, 26 May 1981, p. 5.
20 See Defence and Overseas Policy Working Group of the British Atlantic Committee, *A Global Strategy to Meet the Global Threat* (London: British Atlantic Committee, 1981).
21 See *Western Security: What has Changed? What Should be Done?*, by the Directors of the Research Institute of the German Society for Foreign Policy, the Council on Foreign Relations (New York), the French Institute of International Relations and the Royal Institute for International Affairs (London: RIIA, 1981).
22 See British Atlantic Committee report, op. cit.
23 See H. Morgenthau, 'Alliances in theory and practice', in A. Wolfers (ed.), *Alliance Policy in the Cold War* (Baltimore, Md: Johns Hopkins University Press, 1959), p. 191, and H. Dinerstein, 'Transformation of alliance systems', *American Political Science Review*, vol. 59, no. 3 (1965), p. 599.
24 K. J. Holsti, *International Politics, A Framework for Analysis* (London: Prentice-Hall, 1974), p. 117.
25 *Strategic Survey 1980–1981* (London: IISS, 1981), p. 6.

Selected Bibliography

Allen, R. (1968), *Malaysia: Prospect and Retrospect* (London: Oxford University Press).

Aron, R. (1975), *The Imperial Republic* (London: Weidenfeld & Nicolson).

Barber, J. (1967), *Rhodesia. The Road to Rebellion* (London: Oxford University Press).

Barker, E. (1971), *Britain in a Divided Europe 1945–1970* (London: Weidenfeld & Nicolson).

Barnet, R. J. (1972), *Intervention and Revolution* (London: Paladin).

Bartlett, C. J. (1972), *The Long Retreat* (London: Macmillan).

Baylis, J. (ed.) (1977), *British Defence Policy in a Changing World* (London: Croom Helm).

Baylis, J., Booth, K., Garnett, J., and Williams, P. (1975), *Contemporary Strategy. Theories and Policies* (London: Croom Helm).

Blaxland, G. (1971), *The Regiments Depart* (London: William Kimber).

Blechman, B., and Kaplan, S. (1978), *Force Without War* (Washington, DC: Brookings Institution).

Boardman, R., and Groom, A. J. R. (eds) (1973), *The Management of Britain's External Relations* (London: Macmillan).

Bogdanor, V., and Skidelsky, R. (eds) (1970), *The Age of Affluence 1951–1964* (London: Macmillan).

Boyd, L. V. (1975), *Britain's Search for a Role* (Lexington, Mass.: Saxon House/Lexington Books).

Brown, N. (1967), 'British arms and the switch towards Europe', *International Affairs*, vol. 43, no. 3, pp. 468–82.

Buchan, A. (1966), 'Britain in the Indian Ocean', *International Affairs*, vol. 42, no. 2, pp. 184–93.

Buchan, A. (1967), 'British east of Suez – 1: The problem of power', *RUSIJ*, vol. CXII, no. 647, pp. 209–13.

Calvocoressi, P. (1970), *World Politics Since 1945* (London: Longman).

Calvocoressi, P. (1978), *The British Experience 1945–1975* (London: The Bodley Head).

Carver, M. (1980), *War Since 1945* (London: Weidenfeld & Nicolson).

Clogg, R. (1974), 'Greece and the Cyprus crisis', *The World Today*, vol. 30, no. 9, pp. 364–8.

Crawshaw, N. (1978), *The Cyprus Revolt* (London: Allen & Unwin).

Darby, P. (1973), *British Defence Policy, East of Suez 1947–1968* (London: Oxford University Press).

Eisenhower, D. D. (1966), *The White House Years: Waging Peace 1956–1961* (London: Heinemann).

Frankel, J. (1973), *International Politics. Conflict and Harmony* (Harmondsworth: Penguin).

Frankel, J. (1975), *British Foreign Policy 1945–1973* (London: Oxford University Press).

Freedman, L. (1978), 'Britain's contribution to NATO', *International Affairs*, vol. 54, no. 1, pp. 30–47.

Freedman, L. (1982), 'The war of the Falkland Islands, 1982', *Foreign Affairs*, vol. 61, no. 1, pp. 196–210.

Garnett, J. (1970), 'BAOR and NATO', *International Affairs*, vol. 46, no. 4, pp. 670–81.

Ginwala, F. (1964), 'The Tanganyika mutiny', *The World Today*, vol. 20, no. 3, pp. 93–7.

Gompert, D. C. (1977), 'Constraints of military power: lessons of the past decade', in *The Diffusion of Power*, Adelphi Paper No. 133 (London: International Institute for Strategic Studies), pp. 1–13.

Good, R. C. (1973), *UDI. The International Politics of the Rhodesian Rebellion* (London: Faber).

Greenwood, D. (1976), 'Constraints and choices in the transformation of Britain's defence effort since 1945', *British Journal of International Studies*, vol. 2, no. 1, pp. 5–26.

Gutteridge, W. F. (1965), 'Rhodesia: the use of military force', *The World Today*, vol. 21, no. 12, pp. 499–503.

Gutteridge, W. F. (1969), *The Military in African Politics* (London: Methuen).

Hale, W. M., and Norton, J. D. (1974), 'Turkey and the Cyprus crisis', *The World Today*, vol. 30, no. 9, pp. 368–71.

Hoffmann, S. (1973), 'The acceptability of military force', in *Force in Modern Societies: Its Place in International Politics*, Adelphi Paper No. 102 (London: International Institute for Strategic Studies), pp. 2–13.

Holsti, K. J. (1974), *International Politics, A Framework for Analysis* (London: Prentice-Hall).

Howard, M. (1960), 'Britain's defences: commitments and capabilities', *Foreign Affairs*, vol. 39, no. 1, pp. 81–91.

Howard, M. (1964), 'Military power and international order', *International Affairs*, vol. 40, no. 3, pp. 397–408.

Howard, M. (1977), 'Ethics and power in international policy', *International Affairs*, vol. 53, no. 3, pp. 364–76.

Hunt, D. (1975), *On the Spot* (London: Peter Davies).

IISS (1981a), *Strategic Survey 1980–1981* (London: International Institute for Strategic Studies).

IISS (1981b), *The Military Balance 1981–1982* (London: International Institute for Strategic Studies).

Kellner, P., and Hitchens, C. (1976), *Callaghan. The Road to Number Ten* (London: Cassell).

Knorr, K. (1966), *On the Uses of Military Power in the Nuclear Age* (Princeton, NJ: Princeton University Press).

Leifer, M. (ed.) (1972), *Constraints and Adjustments in British Foreign Policy* (London: Allen & Unwin).

Lellouche, P., and Moisi, D. (1979), 'French policy in Africa: a lonely battle against destabilisation', *International Security*, vol. 3, no. 4, pp. 108–33.

Little, R. (1975), *Intervention. External Involvement in Civil Wars* (London: Martin Robertson).

Macmillan, H. (1971), *Riding the Storm* (London: Macmillan).

Macmillan, H. (1972), *Pointing the Way 1959–1961* (London: Macmillan).

Macmillan, H. (1973), *At the End of the Day* (London: Macmillan).

Mangold, P. (1979), 'Shaba I and Shaba II', *Survival*, vol. XXI, no. 3, pp. 107–15.

Martin, L. (1969), *British Defence Policy: The Long Recessional*, Adelphi Paper No. 61 (London: Institute for Strategic Studies).

Martin, L. (1973), 'The utility of military force', in *Force in Modern Societies: Its Place in International Politics*, Adelphi Paper No. 102 (London: International Institute for Strategic Studies), pp. 14–21.

Mayhew, C. (1967), *Britain's Role Tomorrow* (London: Hutchinson).

Miller, J. D. B. (1974), *Survey of Commonwealth Affairs: Problems of Expansion and Attrition 1953–1969)* (London: Oxford University Press).

Morgenthau, H. J. (1967), 'To intervene or not to intervene', *Foreign Affairs*, vol. 45, no. 3, pp. 425–36.

Nielson, W. A. (1969), *The Great Powers and Africa* (London: Pall Mall).

Northedge, F. S. (1974a), *Descent from Power* (London: Allen & Unwin).

Northedge, F. S. (ed.) (1974b), *The Use of Force in International Relations* (London: Faber).

Neustadt, R. E. (1970), *Alliance Politics* (New York: Columbia University Press).

Owen, D. (1972), *The Politics of Defence* (London: Jonathan Cape).

Pierre, A. J. (1972), *Nuclear Politics* (London: Oxford University Press).

Record, J. (1982), 'The Falklands War', *Washington Quarterly*, vol. 5, no. 4, pp. 43–51.

Reed, B., and Williams, G. (1971), *Denis Healey and the Policies of Power* (London: Sidgwick & Jackson).

Rosecrance, R. N. (1968), *Defence of the Realm* (New York: Columbia University Press).

Rosenau, R. N. (1968), 'The concept of intervention', *Journal of International Affairs*, vol. XXII, no. 2, pp. 165–76.

Schelling, T. C. (1966), *Arms and Influence* (New Haven, Conn., and London: Yale University Press).

Snyder, W. P. (1965), *The Politics of British Defence Policy 1945–1962* (Columbia, Ohio: Ohio State University Press).

Thomas, H. (1967), *The Suez Affair* (London: Weidenfeld & Nicolson).

Vincent, R. J. (1974), *Nonintervention and International Order* (Princeton, NJ: Princeton University Press).

Vincent, R. J. (1975), *Military Power and Political Influence: The Soviet Union and Western Europe*, Adelphi Paper No. 119 (London: International Institute for Strategic Studies).

Vital, D. (1968), *The Making of British Foreign Policy* (London: Allen & Unwin).

Wallace, W. (1977), *The Foreign Policy Process in Britain* (London: Allen & Unwin).

Waltz, K. (1967), *Foreign Policy and Democratic Politics* (London: Longman).

Wilson, H. (1970), *The Labour Government 1964–1970. A Personal Record* (London: Weidenfeld & Nicolson).

Young, C. K. (1969), *Rhodesia and Independence* (London: Dent).

Zartman, I. W. (1968), 'Intervention among developing states', *Journal of International Affairs*, vol. XXII, no. 2, pp. 188–97.

Index

Index